# MADAM PRESIDENT

Sandeep Sahu is a Bhubaneswar-based senior journalist with over three decades of work behind him. He has been reporting for the BBC World Service from Odisha for over twenty-eight years now. Starting out with the leading Odia daily *Sambad* in 1986, he has worked for a host of top local, national and international media houses over the years. He also served as the Odisha correspondent for *Outlook* between May 2018 and December 2021. He writes for a number of national news websites such as Quint, News 18, Firstpost and Federal. He has worked as editorial director of OTV, the No. 1 Odia news channel, and also writes a popular column titled 'Scandeep' on the OTV site. He is among the very few journalists in the state who writes in three different languages: Odia, Hindi and English. Apart from his journalistic work, Sahu has written scripts for scores of documentaries, telefilms and TV serials in Odia, English and Hindi. Sandeep tweets @geminianguddu.

Celebrating 35 Years of
Penguin Random House India

# MADAM PRESIDENT

## The Biography of **Droupadi Murmu**

# SANDEEP SAHU

PENGUIN BOOKS

An imprint of Penguin Random House

PENGUIN BOOKS

USA | Canada | UK | Ireland | Australia
New Zealand | India | South Africa | China

Penguin Books is part of the Penguin Random House group of companies
whose addresses can be found at global.penguinrandomhouse.com

Published by Penguin Random House India Pvt. Ltd
4th Floor, Capital Tower 1, MG Road,
Gurugram 122 002, Haryana, India

Penguin
Random House
India

First published in Penguin Books by Penguin Random House India 2023

Copyright © Sandeep Sahu 2023

Cover photograph © Government of India, 2022, photograph of Droupadi
Murmu, President of India, https://commons.wikimedia.org/wiki/File:Droupadi_
Murmu_official_portrait.jpg,
24/07, under Government Open Data License – India (GODL):
https://data.gov.in/sites/default/files/Gazette_Notification_OGDL.pdf

ISBN 9780143459798

Typeset in Sabon by Manipal Technologies Limited, Manipal
Printed at Thomson Press India Ltd, New Delhi

www.penguin.co.in

# Contents

# 1

# Destiny's Daughter

Call it superstition, or foresight, if you please, but Dillip Kumar Giri is convinced he had seen it coming. Long before Droupadi Murmu became the President of India. Long before she became the Governor of Jharkhand. In fact, long before she even thought of making a career in politics.

Dillip's eyes light up as he goes down memory lane to recall an incident that took place way back in 1995. 'Didi [Droupadi] was teaching nursery classes those days. One day, when she was seated near the door, a lizard fell on her head. She shoved it off but was a little upset about it. She asked me, "What do I do, Dillip?" I told her, "You have a Raja Yoga

1

[Royal Destiny], Didi. Just take two fistfuls of rice in a brass utensil and give it to a Brahmin along with some *dakshina* [monetary offering], and everything will be fine." She simply smiled and did not say anything. I was reminded of that incident every time she took a leap forward in her political career. First, when she became a councillor and the municipal vice chairperson, then a Member of the Legislative Assembly (MLA) and a minister in the Odisha government, then the Governor of Jharkhand, and finally, when she became the President of India,' says the long-time caretaker of Sri Aurobindo Integral Education and Research Centre in Rairangpur, where India's fifteenth President taught from 1994 to 1997.

It is easy to be cynical about the story narrated by Dillip, but there is no denying the role of destiny in the way Murmu's life has panned out in the years since. Those who have known her before she took the plunge into politics aver that this field was farthest from her mind at the time. After serving a four-year stint as a junior assistant in the irrigation department of the Odisha government in the capital city Bhubaneswar, she returned to Rairangpur, her home town, following the death of her eldest daughter Bada Mama, and took up a job as a teacher in the Sri Aurobindo school. By all accounts, she was a good and a very popular teacher; someone who loved her students as much as they loved her. For all one knows, she would have carried on as a teacher for the rest of her life had fate not intervened and brought her into politics.

The countdown for the 1997 elections to the Rairangpur Notified Area Council (NAC) had begun and the Bharatiya Janata Party (BJP), yet to become a force to reckon with in Odisha, was on the lookout for a candidate from Ward No. 2, which was reserved for women. Given the preponderance of tribals in the area, the party was in search of a tribal face to raise its stock in the community. And Murmu fitted the bill perfectly. She was an educated woman who had studied in Bhubaneswar and had served both in the government and as a teacher. But more importantly, she was a Santhal, the dominant tribe in the area. Coincidentally, the school where Murmu taught was located right next to the residence of the then district unit president of the party, Rabindra Mahanta. It was thus natural that she drew the attention of local BJP leaders who frequently gathered at Mahanta's place. Party leader Rajkishore Das, who was eyeing a second successive term as the NAC chairman, first sent an emissary, a fellow teacher of Murmu, to persuade her to join the party and fight the elections. But she was reluctant. Das and other local BJP leaders then approached her and her husband Shyma Charan Murmu, a bank officer, and managed to persuade her. The rest, as they say, is history.

People have slogged for decades to get a ticket to contest an election as an MLA or a Member of

Parliament (MP), not just in the BJP, but in every political party. Some in politics and public life have spent a lifetime without ever being nominated as a candidate in parliamentary or Assembly elections. That Murmu got the BJP ticket to contest the Assembly elections barely three years after joining politics—and the party—was again a matter of providence.

In the run-up to the Assembly elections in Odisha in 2000, the central leadership of the BJP, which was fighting the elections in alliance with the Biju Janata Dal (BJD), had decided that one-third of the sixty-three seats (out of the 147 in the Odisha Assembly) it had got under the seat-sharing formula would have women candidates. But it was a tough ask for the state leadership to find twenty-one women candidates with a reasonable chance of winning. First, the BJP was not yet a major player in the state, where politics at the time was essentially a two-horse race, with the Congress and the BJD (and the Janata Dal earlier) fighting it out between themselves. Second, the party had simply not groomed enough women at the grassroots level for a leadership role and was thus in no position to field twenty-one women candidates and rile male ticket aspirants, who had worked hard for the party for years, in the process. But with her commendable work as a councillor and the vice chairperson of the Rairangpur NAC, Murmu was among the few women in the party who ticked all the boxes and had a realistic chance of winning the election in what was a predominantly tribal constituency. She was an easy pick for the party owing to her stellar record as councillor and vice chairperson of Rairangpur NAC. If anything, the BJP needed her more than she needed the party. She won comfortably and was promptly made a minister of state with independent charge of the commerce and transport department in the first BJD–BJP alliance government headed by Chief Minister (CM) Naveen Patnaik.

Not many politicians have had the good fortune of becoming a minister after winning their very first election as an MLA. Even when they have, they have invariably put in decades of work for the party and at the grassroots level before being considered for a ministerial position, but Murmu was an exception to the rule. She was barely three years old in politics when she became a minister in the Odisha government. This, however, was not something that had happened to her for the first time. She had become the vice chairperson of the Rairangpur NAC after winning her very first election as councillor without any previous experience in politics.

Murmu's first election may have been a cakewalk, but she faced a tough challenge from Rama Chandra Murmu of the Jharkhand Mukti Morcha (JMM) when she fought her second Assembly election in 2004, managing to scrape through by just forty-two votes!

For all one knows, she might have never become the first citizen of the nation had she lost that election. As it happened, she won and devoted herself fully to playing her role as a legislator effectively, winning the Nilakantha Award as the best legislator in 2007—the first woman to win the coveted award. This was a significant entry in her CV which must have been taken into consideration while nominating her as the presidential candidate.

Cut to 2009. Just weeks before the simultaneous Lok Sabha and Assembly elections in Odisha, the BJD announced severance of its alliance with the BJP, leaving the saffron party in a lurch. Soon after the announcement, emissaries from the BJD got in touch with Murmu and her husband and offered her a BJD ticket and a ministerial position to boot. It was a very tempting offer for anyone to reject, but after talking to her mentors in the BJP, Murmu politely declined. Had she taken the bait, she would have certainly become a minister. But as a member of the BJD, there was no way she could have become the President of India because it is a regional party and has never been the ruling party at the Centre though it was part of the National Democratic Alliance (NDA) government in the Vajpayee years.

Murmu lost her eldest son, Laxman, in 2010, when he was barely twenty-six. The cause of his death remains a mystery. Hardly had she recovered from this tragedy when her second son, Biranchi (Sipun), aged twenty-eight, was killed in an accident in 2013. Within a year, she also lost her husband, Shyma Charan Murmu, after a prolonged illness. The three back-to-back tragedies within a span of just four years left her shattered. She went into depression, as anyone in her position would, and seriously considered quitting politics altogether. But a chance visit to the Prajapita Brahma Kumaris Ishwariya Vishwa Vidyalaya centre in Rairangpur saved her from ruin. As she started following the daily ritual of Raja Yoga and meditation, she slowly regained her peace of mind and the desire to live. It was her strong association with the Brahma Kumari organization that helped her get over this turbulent phase in her life and convinced her to spend the rest of her life in the service of humankind, a fact she has acknowledged multiple times over the years.

Her choice as the Governor of Jharkhand was also, in a sense, providential. After winning the 2015 Assembly elections, the BJP chose Raghubar Das, a non-tribal, as the CM of the state since the prominent tribal claimant to the post, Arjun Munda, had lost the election. This did not go down well with the tribals, who constitute as much as 26.21 per cent of the population in the state.[1] The choice of Murmu as Governor was at least partly an effort to assuage the hurt sentiments of the tribals in the state. She rose to the occasion and excelled in her role. At a time when Governors of many states were falling over one another to display loyalty to the ruling party at the Centre, she discharged her responsibility with a quiet dignity and complete non-partisanship, winning the respect of both the ruling party and the Opposition in the process. As we know, it was the exemplary way in which she conducted herself as Governor of Jharkhand for six years that buttressed her claim to be nominated as the presidential candidate of the NDA.

It would, however, be grossly unfair to attribute Murmu's rise to the highest constitutional post in the nation entirely to destiny. To be fair to her, she has earned the position by dint of her dedicated work for the people, her steadfast commitment to the welfare of the most neglected sections of society, and her extraordinary equanimity and fortitude in the face of adversity.

If anything, she has carved her own destiny.

# 2

# The Belated Birthday Gift

'*Droupadi ji se baat karaiye. PM [Prime Minister] baat karna chahte hain* [Connect me to Droupadi Madam. The PM wants to speak to her].' Having been in the thick of politics—and a personal assistant (PA) to Murmu once—Bikash Mahanta was quick to realize the import of what the call meant. 'Please give me five minutes. I am rushing to her place,' he told the man at the other end of the phone and set out on his bike for Murmu's residence, a kilometre or so away.

Just as he entered her premises, the phone rang again. '*Jaldi baat karaiye. PM line par hain* [Connect us to Madam quickly. The PM is on the line],' said the man from the Prime Minister's Office (PMO). '*Haan,*

*Sir, pahunch gaya hun. Bas do minute* [Yes, Sir, I have reached. Please give me two minutes],' Bikash said as he literally ran inside.

It was around 8.30 p.m. Always an 'early-to-bed, early-to-rise' woman since she chose the Brahma Kumari way of life, Murmu had already finished her dinner and was about to go to bed. Bikash handed over the phone to her and watched the expression on her face change. By the end of the conversation, there was little doubt in Bikash's mind that he had guessed it right. As she handed him the phone back, a beaming Murmu broke the news all of Rairangpur —and indeed Odisha—had been eagerly waiting for. 'I am being nominated as the presidential candidate of the NDA.'

'I can't really describe the feeling when I heard that she was going to be the President of the country. And to think that I was the conduit through whom the news had been conveyed . . . It was a magical moment, something that is going to stay with me for the rest of my life,' a visibly elated Bikash told this author.

Soon after the PM, Home Minister Amit Shah, too, spoke to Murmu and congratulated her on her nomination. A short while after that, BJP President J.P. Nadda broke the news to the nation at a press conference in New Delhi.

It is hard to miss the irony. The mobile network failed Murmu precisely at the time when she was about to receive what was easily the most important call in her life. And Bikash had his fifteen minutes of fame as the man who played courier!

Incidentally, Murmu had celebrated, in her typically modest way, her sixty-fourth birthday just the previous day—20 June. Her 'birthday gift' arrived a day late, for sure, but she couldn't possibly have asked for a better one.

Once the announcement was formally made by Nadda in New Delhi, the news of Murmu's nomination as the presidential candidate spread like wildfire. Congratulatory messages, from PM Narendra Modi to the common man, flooded social media, Twitter in particular. 'Smt. Droupadi Murmu Ji has devoted her life to serving society and empowering the poor, downtrodden as well as the marginalized. She has rich administrative experience and had an outstanding gubernatorial tenure. I am confident she will be a great President of our nation,' PM Modi tweeted at 9.52 p.m., shortly after the formal announcement of her candidature.[1]

Other prominent leaders who congratulated her on Twitter were Union Home Minister Amit Shah, Defence Minister Rajnath Singh and External Affairs Minister S. Jaishankar. Union Minister of State for Jal Shakti and Tribal Affairs Bisweswar Tudu, who represents Mayurbhanj, Murmu's home district, in the Lok Sabha said it was a matter of great joy and pride for the district.

Odisha CM Naveen Patnaik, who was away in Rome at the time, lost no time in congratulating her and all but pledging the support of his party, the BJD. 'Congratulations, Smt #DroupadiMurmu on being announced as candidate of NDA for the country's highest office. I was delighted when Hon'ble PM @ narendramodi ji disclosed this with me. It is a proud moment for people of #Odisha,' he tweeted from Rome at 10.49 p.m.[2]

Murmu's phone never stopped ringing through that night. Her daughter Itishree, who was on maternity leave and was staying with her at the time, would pick up the phone and hand it over to her mother. Soon, media persons descended on Murmu's Rairangpur residence in droves. In her first reaction to the media after the announcement, Itishree said: 'That evening (Tuesday), it was raining heavily in Rairangpur and we had a power cut. We got calls from friends and relatives about her selection as the presidential candidate. But after electricity returned, we became doubly sure after watching the news on TV. Then the congratulatory phone calls started. I am feeling very proud.'

'I found it hard to believe it even after watching the news on TV. After all, her name was widely discussed even in 2017. We were given the impression that only the formal announcement remained. But when I heard Nadda ji making the announcement on TV, there was no room left for any doubt. I was ecstatic.

My mother has always believed in working hard for the people without expecting anything in return. I am extremely happy that her hard work has finally been rewarded.'[3]

Even as there was a virtual deluge of phone calls and congratulatory messages on social media, the crowd outside her residence swelled by the minute as people poured in to congratulate her. By daybreak, elite security personnel from the Central Reserve Police Force arrived from Delhi and launched efforts to bring a semblance of order. But it was a tough task, given Murmu's tendency of not disappointing anyone wanting to meet her. Every few minutes, she would come out and greet the constantly surging crowd outside eager to get a glimpse of her.

By morning, the TV cameras, too, converged outside her modest home. Every moment was being beamed live as Murmu met people and accepted their greetings. Just about everyone had their fifteen seconds of fame as reporters waded through the crowd looking for people for the customary byte.

However, the revelries that continued till the wee hours did not affect Murmu's morning routine. A deeply religious person, she went on her temple-hopping spree the next morning. She first went to the Purneswar Shiva Temple and swept the temple floor, as she had done every day, before offering her prayers. In case of any other politician, the act of sweeping floors, gleefully captured and beamed by TV cameras, would have been taken as a photo-op. But the people of Rairangpur knew there was nothing phoney about it. It was all a part of their dear 'Didi's' everyday routine. She then visited the Lord Jagannath and Lord Hanuman temples. Her next stop was the Prajapita Brahma Kumaris Ishwariya Vishwa Vidyalaya and was given a warm reception at the place where she had been a regular for years. She rounded off her temple hopping for the day with a visit to the *jaher*, the open-air prayer place for adivasis.

At around 2.45 p.m., Murmu embarked on her journey to Bhubaneswar en route to New Delhi. The scenes on the way during the 225-kilometre journey had to be seen to be believed. At every town, small and big, delirious people fell over each other to get a glimpse of the woman who they knew was set to become the fifteenth President of India. Despite the heavy security in place, Murmu obliged the people, waving to them. She even tried to get down from the vehicle to accept their greetings at a few places but was prevented from doing so by the security personnel accompanying her.

Even a month after the journey, Narendra Lohar, Murmu's long-time personal chauffeur, can't get over the tumultuous scenes he witnessed right through the five-and-half-hour journey. 'At Jashipur, the people simply laid seize to the road, forcing us to stop. They allowed us to proceed only after the glass windows were lowered and Madam waved and accepted their bouquets and flowers. Some of them even managed to shake hands with her. At Karanjia, there was this woman standing with a few others a little away from the crowd. Madam asked me to halt. She actually wanted to get down but was advised against it by the security people. She then asked me to roll down the windows. The woman came closer to Madam and hugged and kissed her. "You have become big. We can't reach you any more," she said effusively. "Why not? Here I am. Am I not?" replied Madam. It was a very touching moment. I realized that she must have been a very close friend of Madam,' he fondly recollects in a conversation with this author. 'A little further down the road, close to Anandpur town, Madam asked me to stop at a roadside tea stall. Every time we have passed through the road, we have stopped there for tea. Madam herself does not drink tea. But she would order tea for me and whoever else was there in the vehicle. This time though, there was no scope for having tea. Madam just looked out of the window, smiled at the tea shop owner and told him, "Sorry, we can't stop for tea this time." The man was literally in tears and kept standing there with folded hands till we disappeared from sight.' By the end of the conversation, Narendra's eyes, too, are moist. 'No one is happier than me that Madam has become the President of the country. But the only regret I have is I will not be able to drive her vehicle any more,' he signs off.

It was around 8.15 p.m. by the time the cavalcade reached Bhubaneswar, the capital of Odisha. The scenes at the Mahanadi Coalfields Limited guest house, where Murmu was to spend the night, were no less boisterous. With TV channels following her entire journey live, everyone was aware when and where she would arrive. It seemed the whole town had gathered to see—and greet, if possible—the woman who would be President in a few days' time. Friends, family members, past and present political colleagues, other dignitaries and, of course, the media crews, they were all there, eager and expectant. Since the would-be President follows a strict diet regimen that bars her from eating at many places, sisters from the Prajapita Brahma Kumaris Ishwariya Vishwa Vidyalaya centre in the city arrived with her dinner devoid of onion and garlic.

The crowd that had gathered at the Biju Patnaik International Airport to see her off knew that when she would return next, it would be as President of India, with all the attendant paraphernalia. Airport authorities had thoughtfully made special arrangements for a traditional tribal dance performance in her honour at the departure gate.

The days following the announcement of Murmu's name as the presidential candidate spawned a veritable industry around her in the state. Songs were written and recorded hailing her rise to the highest post in the country with 'Rairangpur to Raisina' as the common theme, even though the election and her coronation were still a few weeks away. Social media was awash with posts singing paeans to the 'Daughter of the Soil'. Anyone and everyone who knew her wrote articles in the media—or posts on social media—in praise of her.

The media reached out to her friends, relatives, colleagues and acquaintances, and reporters fanned out to all possible places: her native village, her in laws' village, Rairangpur town, her school and college in Bhubaneswar, and so on, in search of interesting stories from her past. Some of these stories made it to the national media, the most prominent of them being one on the alleged absence of electricity in the would-be President's village. The fact of the matter however was that Murmu's village, Uparbeda, had had power for decades. It was just a cluster of eight to ten houses, including one of her cousins, who had shifted out of the village and settled about a kilometre away, that was yet to be electrified. But who had the time to make that distinction in the frenzy to get a saleable story? Uneasy with the adverse reportage, the administration worked overtime to provide electricity to the 'President's village' as the story was followed up by the media for three or four days. It is, however, a telling commentary on the state of affairs in the country seventy-five years after Independence that it took Murmu's nomination as the presidential candidate for a part of her village to be electrified.

A spate of biographies of the would-be President were conceived and planned as soon as her name was announced as the NDA nominee, at least three of which have already hit the stands. The first off the blocks was Bhavika Maheswari, a thirteen-year-old Class VIII student in Surat, with her book in Hindi *Sangharsh se Shikhar Tak* (From Struggles to the Top). 'My father told some stories about her, which made me curious to know more about her . . . We then tried to find some books on her at the Daryaganj market but we could not find anything there or even on the internet. So, I thought of writing a book on her so that many people like me can read about her. I collected all the information, which I could, from the internet; my father also helped me find some interviews and news about her,' said Bhavika, who had written two books before she took up the biography of Murmu.[4]

As if on cue, Tejaswini Panda, a seventeen-year-old Plus Two student in Odisha, came up with *Rashtrapati Droupadi Murmu: Odia Asmitara Prateeka* (President Droupadi Murmu: A Symbol of Odia Pride) in Odia. The next in line was *Kalinga Kanya Droupadi Murmu* (Daughter of Odisha Droupadi Murmu), a 300-page book in Odia by Pandit Daitari Mahapatra, which was launched by Prof. Ganeshi Lal, the Governor of Odisha, at the Raj Bhavan on 11 October 2022.

With everyone eager to cash in on the 'boom', how could politicians be left behind? Large hoardings with an old picture of Murmu tying a rakhi on the wrist of CM Naveen Patnaik sprung up all over Mayurbhanj. Rairangpur, Murmu's home town, understandably had the largest share of such hoardings. Taking a cue from the hoarding, a rakhi seller at Madhuban square in Baripada town, the district headquarters, put up one in front of his shop to boost sales.

On its part, the BJP organized prayers and lit diyas for Murmu's victory at various temples in Odisha, including the world-famous Jagannath Temple in Puri and Lingaraj Temple in Bhubaneswar, a day before the election on 18 July 2022. The day she was elected, the party organized a massive celebration both in Bhubaneswar and Rairangpur. Frenzied party workers danced their hearts out to the beats of dhols and cymbals at the party headquarters in the state capital, while thousands of laddus were prepared and distributed in the President elect's home town.

At Pahadpur, Murmu's in laws' village, hundreds of men and women congregated at the jaher, the sacred grove of tribals, on 1 July, and bowed their heads before their deity, Marang Buru. In Uparbeda, Murmu's native village, the *dehury*, the village priest, performed puja at the jaher for her victory.

As the results of the presidential election trickled in on 21 July, exactly a month after Murmu was named the NDA candidate, it was obvious that Marang Buru had answered their prayers.

# 3

# The Masterstroke

By all accounts, the nomination of Murmu as the ruling NDA's candidate for President was a political 'masterstroke' by the BJP top brass. It drove a wedge right through the Opposition, sending it into a disarray just as the first tentative moves were afoot to forge a semblance of unity ahead of the 2024 elections. Even parties opposed to the ruling dispensation at the Centre dared not oppose Murmu's candidature for fear of losing tribal votes in the areas of their influence. 'The choice of Murmu ji as the NDA's presidential candidate completely wrongfooted the Opposition. I think the choice of Yashwant Sinha was forced on the Opposition,' BJP vice-president and former MP Jay Panda told this author.

Nowhere was this dilemma more visible than in Maharashtra, where a beleaguered Shiv Sena chief Uddhav Thackeray was fighting a fierce battle for his political survival. Having already announced the support of his party for Yashwant Sinha, the Opposition candidate, Thackeray, who had already lost the CM's chair in a no-holds-barred battle of attrition with the BJP-backed faction in the party led by Eknath Shinde, was left with no choice but to support the NDA candidate when sixteen of his MPs threatened to break off and vote for the former. Murmu's tribal identity provided a ready excuse for the volte face in a state where 9.35 per cent of the population is tribal.[1] It presented a curious case where bitter rivals, locked in a tug of war for supremacy till the announcement was made by Thackeray, ended up voting for the same candidate.

Maharashtra, however, was not the only state where such a thing happened. In what certainly was a first for a presidential election, the pattern was repeated in several states. In Jharkhand, the ruling JMM broke ranks with its alliance partner Congress to pledge its support for Murmu despite the fact that Sinha, the combined Opposition candidate, was a so-called son of the soil.

'Guruji [Jharkhand Mukti Morcha (JMM) supremo CM Shibu Soren] said this is a big opportunity for us. Though our party's vote is not decisive, we must do our bit to ensure that a tribal becomes the President of the country,' explains Supriyo Bhattacharya, the general secretary of the JMM, in a conversation with this author. The fact that Murmu enjoyed an 'excellent relationship' with both Shibu Soren, former CM of Jharkhand, and his son, Jharkhand CM Hemant Soren, when she was the Governor of the state, certainly helped. In the run-up to the presidential election, Murmu had visited Ranchi and met the JMM patriarch, seeking his support. Santhali kinship ties also came into the picture as Hemant, his elder brother Durga (now deceased), and sister Anjali have all married in Mayurbhanj.

However, did the JMM decision not cause strains in its ties with the Congress, its alliance partner? 'No, it did not. Ours is a pre-poll alliance specifically forged for the Assembly elections. Every party is free to decide who to support in the presidential poll. So, why would there be a strain?' asks Bhattacharya. 'We explained to the Congress that it was the only honourable course left for us,' said another party leader, who wished not to be named. As a party committed to upholding the interests of tribals, voting for Sinha, who belongs to the upper caste, would have sent the wrong signal to the people of Jharkhand, he added.

Union Tribal Affairs Minister Arjun Munda, who belongs to Jharkhand, however, believes the JMM did not really have an option. 'As a party wedded to the interests of the tribals, there was no way they could have opposed the candidature of a tribal, and a woman at that,' Munda told this author in a telephonic conversation.

In neighbouring Bihar, Janata Dal (United) chief and CM Nitish Kumar backed Murmu even as he was engaged in a battle of attrition with alliance partner BJP, which ended in a bitter parting of ways a few weeks later. Curiously, Chirag Paswan, Kumar's bête noire and the son of Lok Janshakti Party founder and former Union minister the late Ram Vilas Paswan, also announced his support for the NDA candidate. As did Jitan Ram Manjhi, the founder of the Hindustan Awami Morcha (Secular) (HAM[S]).

There were several other states where the ruling and opposition parties ended up on the same side on the issue of presidential election. Andhra Pradesh presented the most peculiar case where all three major contenders for power—the ruling Yuvajana Sramika Rythu Congress Party (YSRCP), the Telugu Desam Party (TDP) and the BJP—all pledged their support for the NDA candidate. In Karnataka, Janata Dal (Secular) chief and former PM H.D. Deve Gowda, broke off with the Congress and announced his party's support for Murmu, whom he described as 'suitable' and 'noncontroversial'. Bahujan Samaj Party chief Mayawati too backed Murmu, citing the fact that her party was not consulted by the opposition parties before they finalized the name of Sinha as their candidate for the polls. Samajwadi Party (SP) MLA and party chief Akhilesh Yadav's uncle, Shivpal Yadav, went against the party line and announced that he would vote for Murmu. In Punjab, the Shiromani Akali Dal (SAD) put aside its differences with the BJP—it had walked out of the NDA and the Union council of ministers in 2020 in protest against the now repealed farm laws— to announce support for Murmu. 'Murmu not only symbolizes the dignity of womenfolk but also belongs to the very downtrodden and the minority classes for whose cause the great Guru Sahiban made supreme sacrifices,' said a resolution passed by the party's core committee in Chandigarh on 1 July 2022.[2]

The BJD, the ruling party in Odisha, of course, was the first off the blocks in announcing support for Murmu's candidature without even waiting for a formal request from the BJP. In fact, party supremo Naveen Patnaik did not stop at just pledging the support of his party for Murmu; he urged other parties in the state to back the 'daughter of the soil'. Taking to Twitter, the BJD boss and Odisha CM said on 22 June 2022, 'Appeal all members of the Odisha Legislative Assembly, cutting across party lines, to extend unanimous support to elect the daughter of

#Odisha – Smt #DraupadiMurmu – to the country's highest office.'

His appeal drew an immediate response from Makaranda Muduli, the independent MLA from Rayagada in Koraput district, who met the CM and pledged his support to Murmu. (Amused observers wondered why the 'independent' MLA met the CM to pledge his support when he could have simply announced it in public? Interestingly, the announcement on his support was made not by him but by the Chief Minister's Office!) Despite being aware of the stated position of the Congress, Patnaik spoke to Narasingha Mishra, the leader of the Congress Legislature Party, to seek the party's support and then sent his trusted lieutenant, BJD organization secretary Pranab Prakash Das, to follow up. Simultaneously, he directed his ministers and senior vice-presidents of the party to meet the Pradesh Congress Committee (PCC) president, Congress MLAs and CPI (M) MLA Laxman Munda individually.

As proof of his commitment to getting Murmu elected, the BJD boss sent two Cabinet members— Jagannath Saraka and Tukuni Sahu—to New Delhi to sign her nomination papers when she filed her nomination on 24 June. As if on cue, an old picture of Murmu tying a rakhi on Naveen's hand from 2000, when she was a minister in the Patnaik government, resurfaced soon after the Odisha CM announced his unstinted support for her. Murmu reciprocated in equal measure thanking her 'brother' for 'keeping his rakhi promise' when she visited Odisha on 8 July and met legislators to seek their vote for the election.

During her interaction with BJD MLAs and MPs in the Odisha Assembly on 8 July, she got emotional and said, 'As Subhadra (sister), I had tied rakhi on the wrist of Jagannath (Patnaik). Before the sister could ask for anything, the brother declared his support for her. I am indebted to him (Patnaik) for this good gesture towards this daughter of Odisha.'[3]

Both during the interaction with the BJD legislators as well as the reception at the BJP office that followed, she played on the 'daughter of the soil' theme, coined by Naveen Patnaik, to the hilt. She said all the MLAs were her brothers and sisters. 'I have worked with most of them. Those who became members after I left are also my brothers and sisters. I may not know them personally, but technology has brought all of us close to each other. I seek the support of all my brothers and sisters. Please make sure that not a single vote is wasted,' she said, addressing the legislators.

The CM hosted a lunch for the would-be President at his residence, Naveen Nivas, in the presence of Union Minister Gajendra Singh Shekhawat and leader of the BJD Parliamentary Party Pinaki Misra where the vegetarian fare laid out included the best of Odia cuisine like baigan bhaja, alu bharta and badi chura.

The BJD president followed it up by sending emissaries to leaders of all other parties to persuade them to vote for Murmu. The BJP, the main opposition party in the state, of course, needed no persuasion since she was the party candidate. The other major opposition party in the state, the Congress, made it clear that it would back the combined opposition candidate Yashwant Sinha. But with just nine MLAs in its stable, the party knew its vote would not make a big dent in Murmu's winning prospects.

Asked if the party should not have voted for the 'daughter of the soil', the leader of the Congress Legislature Party (CLP), Narasingha Mishra, quipped: 'By that reckoning, why are the BJP and the JMM not supporting Yashwant Sinha, who is a "son of the soil", in Jharkhand? We will not back her candidature as she believes in the ideology of the BJP and RSS. The people of this ideology killed Mahatma Gandhi and the Congress can never support it,' he said.[4]

Canny politician that he is, Naveen Patnaik lost no time and went out of his way to garner support for Murmu, so much so that it appeared she was his party's candidate rather than the BJP's. Barely an hour after the announcement, he tweeted that he was 'delighted' when PM Modi disclosed her name during their meeting days before he left for Rome on what was only the second foreign trip during his twenty-three-year reign as the CM. Interestingly, however, he had told media persons in New Delhi immediately after emerging from the meeting with Modi that there was no discussion on the presidential election during his talks with the PM. His tweet from Rome, which suggested that he was privy to the BJP's decision to nominate Murmu, was, therefore, taken with a pinch of salt by those who were following the political developments leading up to the presidential election. Speculation was rife in media and political circles in Odisha. Several questions were raised, but no answers were forthcoming. Did Naveen know about Murmu's candidature before her name was announced? If he did, why did he tell the media immediately after meeting the PM that the presidential election did not figure in his talks with Modi? Was he asked to keep it a secret till the formal announcement was made? Or was he just trying to make a virtue out of a necessity by backing Murmu and score some political brownie points in the process? Senior BJP leader and party's national vice-president Jay Panda, for one, is sure it was the latter.

One would never really know what transpired behind the scenes. BJD leaders, of course, were emphatic that the PM had 'consulted' the BJD supremo on Murmu's name before it was made public. Some political observers in the state believed that Naveen may have been told about a list of prospective candidates, including Murmu, by the PM. But a top BJP leader from the state avers Naveen had no inkling of Murmu's candidature. 'Do you think he would have left for Rome at such an important juncture if he had known about it beforehand?' he asks. Another local BJP leader feels he might have got an inkling about Murmu's impending nomination when the customary police and legal verification process was initiated by the Centre before the formal announcement.

Whether or not he knew about it beforehand, Naveen seized the opportunity to derive as much political mileage as he could from Murmu's nomination. Once she was elected, Naveen, who has difficulty speaking in Odia even after twenty-three years as CM, wrote an article—in Odia, mind you—titled 'E Matira Kanya' (The Daughter of this Soil), which was gleefully published by all Odia newspapers in their editorial pages. This was a first in his over two-decade-long stint as the CM. Naveen, along with all BJD MPs, also met the President elect a day before her swearing-in on 25 July. 'I am so pleased and honoured that a daughter of Odisha has been chosen to be the President of India,' he said after meeting the President elect.

Curiously, the state unit of the BJP played along without a murmur, perhaps mindful of the fact that the BJD's votes—it has twelve MPs in the Lok Sabha, nine in the Rajya Sabha and 113 MLAs in the Odisha Assembly—would tilt the scales decisively in favour of its candidate.

The Congress said it was the fear of losing the tribal vote that had forced Naveen to back Murmu's candidature. And it may well have a point there. Murmu's nomination for the top constitutional post in the country had created tremendous enthusiasm among the tribals in the state, where they constitute 22.85 per cent of the population.[5] While the BJD has swept every poll since 2000, it has been a mixed bag for the party in the tribal pockets, with the BJP having a substantial support base in these areas. Nowhere is this more evident than in Mayurbhanj, where over 58 per cent of the people are tribals and six of the seven MLAs are from the BJP. It was thus important for the ruling party to create the right vibes among the tribals and deny the BJP complete sway over the tribal vote ahead of the 2024 elections. The political significance of the choice of the two leaders to represent the party at Murmu's nomination was not lost on anyone. While Saraka is a tribal leader from south Odisha, Sahu is a woman.

While the final call on the presidential nomination was clearly taken by the 'Big Two' in the BJP—PM Modi and Home Minister Shah—there are several others who are believed to have played a role in pushing her case. The most prominent of them, of course, is Union Minister for Education and Skill Development Dharmendra Pradhan, the pre-eminent leader of the Odisha BJP and a close confidante of the Big Two. 'As someone who had the opportunity of observing things up close in the run-up to the presidential election, I can tell you that Dharmendra Pradhan played a key role in Murmu's nomination,' Golak Mohapatra, a general secretary of the party's state unit, told this author. The fact that Pradhan was with Murmu right through her maiden, two-day visit to her home state in November 2022 appears to corroborate this view. But another general secretary of the state unit attributes the nomination of Murmu for the top post to Girish Chandra Murmu, the PM's trusted officer who is now the Comptroller and Auditor General of India (CAG). Murmu, a native of Mayurbhanj like Murmu, has enjoyed excellent relations with the PM since his days in Gujarat when he served as the Principal Secretary to CM Modi.

That there was no unity of purpose or a clear strategy among the opposition parties had become abundantly clear even before Sinha's name was announced as their candidate for the presidential election. At a meeting of seventeen opposition parties convened by her in New Delhi on 15 June, Trinamool Congress Party (TMC) president and West Bengal CM Mamata Banerjee proposed the names of National Conference patriarch and former Jammu and Kashmir (J&K) CM Farooq Abdullah and Nationalist Congress Party (NCP) chief Sharad Pawar as prospective candidates. Both, however, were quick to decline the offer. Abdullah said he still had 'a lot more active politics' ahead of him and wanted to contribute to navigating J&K, now a Union territory, through the 'critical juncture' it was passing through.[6] On his part, Pawar did not offer a reason for declining the offer. 'I sincerely appreciate the leaders of [the] opposition parties for suggesting my name as a candidate for the election of the President of India, at the meeting held in Delhi. However I [would] like to state that I have humbly declined the proposal of my candidature,' he said on Twitter.[7]

When Pawar convened the next round of meeting to finalize an opposition candidate, Mamata, apparently, peeved over the absence of any reference to the earlier meeting convened by her in the invite sent out by the NCP chief, decided to skip it and sent her nephew Abhishek Banerjee instead.

With both Pawar and Abdullah having opted out of the race, opposition leaders next approached Gopal Gandhi, the grandson of Mahatma Gandhi and former Governor of West Bengal, but he, too, declined the offer, saying, 'Opposition's presidential candidate should generate national consensus. There will be others who will do this far better than I.'[8]

The confabulations among the opposition parties continued even as the last date for the filing of nomination drew closer. After hectic parleys, the combined Opposition finally zeroed in on the name of Sinha as its candidate, reportedly at the behest of TMC.

Even as the discussions continued among opposition leaders and parties, the BJP kept its cards close to its chest. Several names were doing the rounds as the prospective NDA candidate for President. Among them were Kerala Governor Arif Mohammad Khan, former Union minister Mukhtar Abbas Naqvi, former Punjab CM Capt. Amarinder Singh and, of course, Murmu. The fact that Naqvi resigned from the Union council of ministers on the eve of the presidential election and was not nominated to the Upper House strengthened speculation that he could be the NDA's pick for the top job. The prospects of Khan and Naqvi appeared bright as it was seen as the BJP extending an olive branch to the Muslims of the country—just as it had done in 2002 by picking aerospace scientist Dr A.P.J. Abdul Kalam as its presidential candidate—who have no love lost with the saffron party due the party's ideological roots and Hindutva agenda.

The Opposition was clearly caught off guard when the BJP announced the name of Murmu, who did not appear to be the front runner among those being discussed as the possible candidate, as its official nominee. Several parties in the opposition camp, mindful of the adverse political fallout of opposing an adivasi, started having a rethink on their decision to

back Sinha. Why, even Mamata, the prime mover of
the efforts to put up a consensus opposition candidate,
did a volte face of sorts after the BJP/NDA announced
the name of Murmu as its candidate. 'Had BJP
informed us that they will make an Adivasi woman
their Presidential candidate, we could also have tried
(for consensus) on it,' she said.[9]

In essence, Mamata's statement was a tacit
admission that the BJP had outsmarted it by keeping
its choice under wraps and the Opposition guessing.

When Murmu's candidature was announced, the
NDA was marginally short of the numbers required to
win the election. But after the announcement, support
for her came pouring in from unexpected quarters. The
Opposition did not help its cause with some rather
tasteless, undignified comments on Murmu by some
of its leaders. Her rival, Sinha, dubbed her a 'rubber
stamp' who he said would not be able to uphold and
protect the Constitution.[10]

Congress leader Ajoy Kumar said Murmu represents
a 'very evil philosophy'.[11]

The BJP predictably pounced on the comment to
seek an unqualified apology from the Congress for
this 'insult' not just to her but to the entire adivasi
community. BJP members created a ruckus on the issue
in the Odisha Assembly. Hardly had the furore over
Kumar's statement subsided when RJD leader Tejashwi
Yadav, who became the deputy CM of Bihar shortly

thereafter, said rather derisively that the country did not deserve a 'statue' in the Rashtrapati Bhavan whose voice had 'never been heard'.[12]

One would never really know if these comments influenced voting in the presidential election in any manner. But when the results were announced on 20 July, it became clear that the Opposition had failed miserably to keep its flock together. Since whips are not issued by parties during the election for President and voting is through a secret ballot, there was no way of identifying—and 'punishing'—the culprits. While Murmu's victory was never in doubt once the BJD and YSRCP declared their support for her, the margin of victory surprised many even in the NDA camp. She got 6,76,803 votes (nearly 64 per cent) against the 3,80,177 polled by her rival Sinha. The huge margin of victory could be attributed, at least partly, to massive cross-voting in favour of the NDA candidate. As many as 126 Opposition MLAs and at least seven MPs reportedly defied their party line and voted for Murmu. Assam reported the maximum number of cross-voting. While the NDA has seventy-nine MLAs in the 126-member state Assembly, Murmu received 104 votes out of the 124 who voted (two members abstained), indicating that at least twenty-five members from the Opposition had voted for her. Madhya Pradesh reported the next highest number of cross-voting with nineteen, followed by sixteen in Maharashtra, ten each in Gujarat and Jharkhand, eight in Bihar, six in Congress-ruled Chhattisgarh and three in Goa. In Murmu's home state of Odisha, Congress MLA Mohammed Mouqim openly admitted that he had voted for Murmu, using the 'daughter of the soil' argument to justify his decision.

By all accounts, Murmu's tribal identity did tilt the scales decisively in her favour, as is obvious from the pattern of voting in states with a large proportion of tribal votes. While there were other claimants for the nomination in the BJP like Union Tribal Affairs Minister and three-time CM of Jharkhand Arjun Munda and his predecessor in the Union cabinet Jual Oram, who, incidentally, is also from Odisha, what apparently clinched the issue in Murmu's favour was the fact that she is a woman. Senior Odisha BJP leader Sajjan Sharma adds a third dimension to the selection of Murmu: region. 'Representation to all zones has been a major policy formulation of the NDA government since 2014. If you see the two presidential elections during the Modi regime, you will find a definite pattern to it. In the 2017 election, the presidential candidate, Ramnath Kovind, was from the north (Uttar Pradesh), while the candidate for the post of vice-president, M. Venkaiah Naidu, was from the south (Andhra Pradesh). This time, the President is from the east (Oidsha) while the vice-president, Jaydeep Dhankar, is from the west (Rajasthan),' he told this author in an interview.

Some commentators have also pointed to the fact that she is an unabashed practitioner of Hindu rituals even as she holds on to her tribal roots to surmise that this was one of the major considerations in the BJP opting for her. They are of the view that Murmu's nomination was, in a way, an attempt by the BJP to puncture the left-liberal narrative, supported by a section of tribals, that Adivasis are a distinct religious entity and are not Hindus.

But prominent Santhal leader and former Jharkhand CM Babulal Marandi, currently the leader of the BJP Legislature Party in the state Assembly, sees no contradiction in the party's presidential candidate embodying the best of both Hindu and tribal traditions in her. 'Those who say tribals are not Hindus are either ignorant about what a Hindu means or are saying so out of political considerations. There is no prescribed scripture, way of worship, rituals or belief systems in Hinduism. Everyone is free to follow his or her own path. Hence, it is possible to be a true Hindu while holding on to one's tribal origins without one encroaching on the other,' he told this author in an interview.

The debate on whether tribals are Hindus is unlikely to end anytime soon. But there is little doubt that in choosing Murmu as its presidential candidate, the BJP has tried to expand its footprint in the tribal homeland of east and central India. Significantly, almost all the states with a significant tribal population in this vast region—Jharkhand, Odisha, Chhattisgarh, West Bengal, Andhra Pradesh and Telangana—are ruled by the Opposition. As is clear from the ecstatic reaction of Meghalaya CM Conrad Sangma, whose father and former Lok Sabha Speaker Purno A. Sangma had fought and lost the presidential election in 2012, Murmu's nomination created a positive vibe among the large population of tribals in north-east India. Describing it as 'historic', Sangma said: 'At this point in time, I remember my late father, who was somebody who truly believed in this and was the person who laid the foundation for this idea and this thought. He would have been the proudest person in the country today.'[13] The senior Sangma, whose candidature had been proposed by the BJD and the AIADMK and backed by the BJP, had eventually lost to the Congress-led United Progressive Alliance (UPA) candidate, the late Pranab Mukherjee.

There had been an attempt to anoint a tribal as the President of India earlier too. In 1992, the BJP and other parties had backed George Gilbert Swell, a Khasi tribal from eastern Meghalaya, as their presidential candidate, but he lost to the Congress candidate, Dr Shankar Dayal Sharma. Munda told this author that his party (the BJP) had proposed the name of noted academician Dr Ram Dayal Munda as a consensus presidential candidate in 2012, but it was not accepted by the ruling Congress party, which chose Sri Mukherjee as its nominee.

While the earlier attempts to get a tribal elected to the highest constitutional post had all been a losing cause, this was the first time a tribal had a realistic chance at winning the election, given the numbers in the two houses of Parliament and the state Assemblies. Murmu's name was among those considered for the post by the BJP/NDA in 2017 too, but the ruling dispensation eventually settled for Kovind, a Dalit (Scheduled Caste or SC) leader from Uttar Pradesh, the state with the highest population in the country, as part of the BJP's outreach to one of the most oppressed and neglected sections of society. The fact that she was only fifty-nine and thus 'too young' for the exalted post was also a factor believed to have worked against her at the time. It is another matter that she still had the honour of becoming the youngest President the country has seen when she was sworn-in five years later.

After losing the presidential election in 2012, P.A. Sangma had predicted that India will soon have a tribal President.[14] Exactly ten years later, his prophesy has come true. That it took seventy-five years after India's independence for a tribal to rise to the highest political office in the country is not exactly a great advertisement for Indian democracy. But there can be no two opinions about the fact that the coronation of the first tribal as President of India has enhanced India's credentials as a functioning democracy and an inclusive society. Murmu herself acknowledged as much when she said, during her speech after being sworn-in: 'It is a tribute to the power of our democracy that a daughter born in a poor family in a remote tribal area can reach the highest constitutional position in India.'[15]

The world has certainly taken note of it, as is evident from reports in the foreign media. To cite just one example, the *Washington Post*, in a report published on 21 July, a day after the election, said: 'But in a democracy often driven by caste, religion and regional identities, Murmu's elevation could reverberate far beyond her largely ceremonial office, particularly among the 100 million tribal people in India who have long sat at the foot of the country's socioeconomic order—and who have been assiduously wooed, critics note, by a BJP that has been trying to expand its appeal beyond its traditional base of upper-caste Hindus.'[16]

While the choice of Murmu for the post has been hailed by most people, sceptics feel it is mere tokenism. They wonder whether it would make a qualitative difference to the lot of the tribals, who lag far behind other sections of Indian society in terms of almost all development indices. As per the 2011 Census, the latest one for which comprehensive figures are available, 45 per cent of tribals in India are below poverty line (BPL) as against 26 per cent for others. They have a literacy rate of just 59 per cent compared to 74 per cent overall. The figures for other indices like infant mortality rate (IMR), anemia among women, underweight children, and so on, make for equally depressing reading.[17]

The jury is still out on the issue. Union Minister Munda, for one, believes it will make a difference in the plight of tribals since Murmu's anointment has raised the expectations of the community which, in turn, would create an obligation on the government that nominated her to do more for this neglected section of Indian society.

And if Murmu's six-year stint as Governor of Jharkhand is anything to go by, there is a lot that can be done even within the limitations of the otherwise 'ceremonial' post if the will is there. As Governor of Jharkhand, she had used her constitutional powers to stall a Bill that was perceived as anti-tribal and helped prevent a secessionist movement building up among tribals from going out of hand.

# 4

# 'Puti' to Droupadi

The south-west monsoon had set in, but there was no sign of rain in Uparbeda village and the surrounding areas for days on end. In keeping with Santhali practices, Biranchi Narayan Tudu, like others in the village, had placed an earthen pot, called *puti* in local parlance, beneath the banyan tree on the backyard to propitiate the rain gods. About a week after the puti was placed, on 20 June 1958 to be precise, there was a new arrival in the family in the shape of a skinny baby girl. As if on cue, the rains arrived almost immediately after the birth of the child.

Tudu promptly named his newborn daughter 'Puti' in grateful acknowledgement of the role it had played in bringing rains and a daughter for him in a family of predominantly male members. In the years that followed, the name Puti underwent several changes to finally become Droupadi, the woman the Indian nation now knows as its incumbent President. 'In Santhali tradition, when a girl child is born, she is given the name of her paternal grandmother so that the name never dies and is kept alive. In keeping with this tradition, I was named Puti by my parents. But the teachers in my school, who mostly hailed from the coastal areas of the state, did not like the name and changed it first to Durpadi, then Dorpadi, Durpati and finally Droupadi,' the President told journalist and author Dr Iti Samanta in a video interview when she was Governor of Jharkhand. After her marriage to Shyam Charan Murmu, she acquired her husband's surname, as is the custom, to be known as Murmu.[1]

Delha Soren, Murmu's senior in college and a lifelong friend, recounts an interesting anecdote involving her name from her school days which she says was narrated to her by Murmu herself. During a class examination, while Murmu was in middle school, the students were asked to write the other names by which some mythological characters from Hindu scriptures were known by. Murmu had no problem with the other names: 'Dharmaraj' for Yudhisthir, 'Gandivdhari' for Arjun, and so on, but stumbled at the name 'Yagyanseni'. Watching her scratching her head, the teacher asked her, 'Why don't you write the answer?' 'Sir, I have written down the answers to all other questions, but don't know any other name for Yagyanseni,' Murmu replied nervously. 'If you can't recollect one, why don't you write down your own name?' the teacher said with a smile. Murmu did as was told. It was only later that she realized 'Yagyanseni' was another name for her namesake from the Mahabharata.

In most homes in the largely patriarchal Indian society, the birth of a girl is not celebrated with the same fervour as that of a boy. Even in this age and time, female foeticide is prevalent, even rampant, in many parts of the country, as reflected in the abysmal nationwide gender ratio of 1000:933.[2] Nor does the discrimination end at birth; it continues unabated for the rest of her life. But that is not the case in the egalitarian tribal society. Here, the birth of a girl child is as much a cause for celebration as the arrival of a son. No wonder the sex ratio in tribal society is a healthy 1000:990.[3]

In true tribal tradition, therefore, Biranchi Narayan, who already had a son named Bhagat, rejoiced at the birth of a daughter. A marginal farmer with a small land holding, Biranchi did not study much beyond primary school. But he was determined to give his daughter the best possible education. 'He would often say that he would not hesitate to sell off his meagre land holding, if need be, to send his daughter to college and university,' Murmu's teacher in middle English (ME) school, Basudev Behera, told this author. With this kind of parental backing, it was perhaps natural that the young Murmu developed a passion for education, something that earned for her the honour of becoming the first girl in her village to join college. This was to be the first of the many firsts she would achieve in her life later: the first woman from her area to become a minister in the Odisha government, the first woman to win the coveted Nilakantha Award as the best legislator in the Odisha Assembly, the first woman—and the first tribal—to be appointed Governor of Jharkhand, the first person born after Independence to become President, the first from Odisha to rise to the highest constitutional post in the country and, of course, the first tribal in Raisina Hill.

Born as she was into a poor family, life was not easy for the young Murmu. She would walk to school barefoot, as she could not afford footwear. She had to manage the whole year with just two pairs of dress, which she wore alternately after washing. She also had to do all domestic chores: washing utensils, sweeping the floor, drawing water from the well, cleaning the cowshed, and so on, even as she pursued her passion for education. Her grandmother would call her out at 4 a.m. to help her at the *dhinki* (old-style wooden lever used to remove husk from rice in the Indian countryside). 'Do you think you would go to heaven by simply studying?' she would tell young Murmu. The old lady would admonish her for using a kerosene lamp, called *dibiri* in local parlance, saying, 'What are you doing in school then? Why don't you study there? Do you even know how much kerosene costs?' But determined as she was to pursue her education and secure in the knowledge that she had the backing of her father, Murmu would ignore the admonishment of her grandmother and carry on.

As the exams neared, 'Basu Sir' held extra classes for students in the evenings after school hours. Electricity was yet to reach the area and a dibiri, which cost about Rs 30 at the time, was not something either the school or the students could afford. So, they had to manage with a makeshift dibiri made out of inkpots, glass medicine bottles or tin pots with torn clothes used as wick. 'Murmu's father would drop her to school in the evening and would come again at 9 p.m. to fetch her,' says Basu Sir.

Nothing would stop her from going to school. 'I can't recollect one occasion when she missed school. Once, there was a heavy downpour, which flooded the road leading from her home to the school. The water rose to a height of about four feet in a nullah she had to cross to reach school. Only the headmaster and me, besides four or five boy students, had managed to reach school. Just as we were thinking of calling off classes for the day, I was stunned to see Droupadi arrive at school all drenched. I asked her, "How did you come?" "I swam," she replied coolly. While crossing the nullah, she was holding her school bag aloft to make sure it did not get wet. That was the level of her commitment to education,' Behera says.

The genial teacher says he never imagined his student would become the President of the country one day. 'The most I had expected was she would complete her matriculation and would become, given her passion for education, a teacher, like me,' Behera says with a smile.

Tankadhar Mandal, her classmate in ME school, says she was very good in studies and always stood first in her class. 'As per a long-observed tradition in the school, the student who stood first in class was made monitor of the class. Thus, Droupadi was set to become the monitor. But some boys had reservations about a girl becoming the monitor. They opposed her, saying she would be unable to discharge her responsibilities as monitor properly. That is when Basu Sir stepped in and put his foot down,' he says. Distressed at the lack of confidence in her, Murmu asked Basu Sir, 'Can't I become the monitor?' 'Why not? You will do a better job than any boy,' the teacher said. Murmu duly became monitor and gave a very good account of herself in what was an early indication of her leadership quality and her determination to fight gender discrimination.

Murmu soon won over the sceptics with her love and affection. 'She was always respectful towards her elders and treated her classmates like her own brothers and sisters. I can't recollect one occasion when she had a tiff with anyone during the entire period she was in school,' an admiring Bishweswar Mohanta, her headmaster in ME school, says of his former student in an interview with this writer.

Even as a child, she was never afraid of speaking her mind, Mohanta says. 'While teaching, we teachers would often ask the students, "Did you understand what I just said?" While others would nod their heads or just keep quiet, Droupadi would say, without any inhibition, "No, Sir. I couldn't. Will you please explain again?"' he says. 'This was a very noteworthy trait in her character.'

Her love for education, however, did not mean that Murmu missed out on having fun. 'Whenever there was a festival in the village, she would abandon her normal attire of skirt and blouse and ask me for a saree and ornaments, wear them and participate in merry-making. After returning from school, she would finish the household chores like drawing water from the well and washing utensils in a jiffy before slipping out to play with children of her age,' Jaba Tudu (eighty-two), Murmu's stepmother, reminisces while speaking to this author. 'There was no segregation between boys and girls at the playground. They would play together, and Droupadi would often beat her male playmates at a game,' she adds. 'She could run fast, so fast that even girls much older than her could not keep pace.'

Tapati Mandal, a close friend who studied with Murmu from Class I to VII, fondly recalls the wonderful childhood days they spent together. 'We spent most of our time together; not just in school but even after that. She considered my home her own. The best thing about her is even after she became a minister and a Governor, she did not change one bit. Even now, we are buddies; she makes it a point to meet me whenever she visits her village,' she says.[4]

During vacations, Murmu would often visit her maternal uncle's place nearby and have fun with her uncles and cousins. 'Since she is my only niece, she was loved by everyone in the family. My mother would cook a variety of dishes for her. But she loved rice and vegetables more than anything else. She would spend most of her time playing with girls in the village. Wherever she would see me, she would come rushing, saying "Mamu, Mamu",' her maternal uncle Dasamat Marandi reminisces, as quoted in *Rashtrapati Droupadi Murmu: Odia Asmitara Prateeka*.

Murmu was also a good singer. 'There was this man named Ananda Giri, who was the school president, besides being a folk singer. He used to come to the school every Saturday to teach the nuances of singing to the students. Murmu had a sweet voice and she picked up the basics of singing real fast. Soon, she started singing well-known Odia bhajans like "Ahe Nila Saila", "Ahe Dayamaya" and "Ki Sundara Aha". So sweet was her singing that people passing by the school stopped to listen to her,' a beaming Basu Sir says.

During breaks, while other girls would gossip and have fun, Murmu would collect kharang grass from the nearby jungle, dry them and weave brooms out of them to sweep the classrooms and the school veranda. Over a period, she acquired an enviable expertise in making brooms and taught the skill to other girls. Once, she saw a teacher who had shaved his head as per local custom on losing a family member use his cap to wipe the blackboard clean in the absence of a duster. The next day, Murmu presented three dusters, neatly knitted out of torn cloths, to her teacher. She was very particular about cleanliness, not just her own but also of the surroundings in which she moved about. She would clean the classroom every day and apply cow dung paste on the earthen floor whenever it got dirty.

Charity, fellow feeling and respect for elders were important traits in Murmu's character even when she was young. 'Since my home was a little far from the school, she would often invite me to her home during lunch break to have *pakhala* (fermented rice which is the staple of most Odias in rural areas), and vegetables,' recalls her classmate in primary school,

Gobinda Majhi. 'While playing, others would laugh and make fun if someone fell down. But Murmu would rush to him or her, nurse the wound, if any, and console him or her,' he adds in an interview to Anuj Das of Kanak News.[5]

She would not allow the school peon, who was a teacher once, to sweep the floor and volunteered to do the job herself. 'He is such an elderly person and has taught our seniors. We address him as "Kaka" (uncle). He shouldn't be sweeping floors,' she would say. She would make it a point to meet her teachers and pay her respects to them whenever she returned to her village even after holding high political and constitutional positions. While she was Governor of Jharkhand, she once invited all her former teachers from primary and ME school, touched their feet in a humbling gesture of 'Guru Vandana' (worship of teacher) in grateful acknowledgement of their contribution in her life and presented them dresses, pens and bouquets.

To prepare students properly for the scholarship examination in Class VII, Basu Sir used to conduct weekly examinations for them. Murmu was a bright prospect and hence the school authorities paid special attention to her. Since she did not have a compass, she was given one from the school stock by the headmaster Bishweswar Mohanta. But immediately after the examinations were over, she offered to return the compass to the school. 'Why are you returning it? You will need it in future too,' said the headmaster. But Murmu was politely insistent. 'Sir, I did not win it as a prize. You had given it to me from the school stock. The students who come after me will need it. I will manage when I go to high school,' she told the headmaster.

Murmu's father could not afford to buy her new books. Before a new session started, he would request the parents of those passing out for their old books to be used by his daughter. But some of the books thus acquired were so tattered that they would need glue to stick the pages together to prevent further damage. But even the lowly glue was a luxury poor Murmu could ill afford. So, she had to make do with hot, boiled rice instead. Once she was promoted to the next class, she would make it a point to return the old books to the school so that others could use them.

Poverty and deprivation, however, never affected Murmu. She was happy with what she had and had no complaints and regrets about life. 'I was happy since all of us were poor and had no one to compare ourselves with. It was only when I left my village and saw the world outside that I realized the world of difference existing between the haves and the have-nots,' Murmu would tell Dr Samanta in the video interview much later in life.

Even as a child, Murmu was inspired by the lives and deeds of great men. Tapati Mandal, her erstwhile classmate in school, recalls an anecdote from their school days that suggests her now famous buddy perhaps knew even then that she was cut out for greatness. 'The teacher had asked the students to recite a poem. As usual, Murmu was the first to volunteer. The poem she recited was an Odia translation of Robert Frost's famous English poem "Stopping by Woods on a Snowy Evening". While teaching a chapter on Jawaharlal Nehru earlier, the teacher had told the students that it was the favourite of India's first Prime Minister and was famously found on Nehru's table after his death in 1964. As she sat down after reciting the famous last line "Miles to go before I sleep", I mockingly asked her: "Do you want to become a leader like Nehru?" "Why not?" she replied without batting an eyelid. I did not take it very seriously then. But when I think of this incident in hindsight, I wonder if she already had an inkling that she was destined for greatness,' Tapati reminisces.

Murmu's octogenarian former headmaster Bishweswar Mohanta is a frail man, barely able to walk now. But his eyes light up at the mere mention of his ex-student who has risen to the highest post in the country. 'I cannot thank the school management enough for appointing me the headmaster and giving me the opportunity to proclaim to the world that the President of India was once a student of mine,' the proud teacher signs off.

# 5

# Bhubaneswar Beckons

Nestled amid hills, Uparbeda is a sprawling village of some 500-odd households with a population of about 3000, a majority of them tribals. The upper primary school in the village was established as early as 1902. But the nearest high school was in Badampahar, some 10 kilometres from Uparbeda. Though young Murmu had never ventured outside her village, her sight was set far beyond her immediate surroundings.

One day, Kartik Majhi, a minister in the Odisha government, was scheduled to address a public meeting in Rairangpur, the nearest town. Hailing from Uparbeda, he happened to be the elder cousin of Murmu's father. On hearing about the meeting, young

Murmu cajoled her father to take her to Rairangpur. Biranchi thought his daughter was curious to see what it was like when someone she knew addressed a meeting and agreed to her request. Little did he imagine at the time what would transpire at the meeting.

Just as the minister was winding up his speech, he saw Murmu climbing on to the stage. Waving her Class VII certificate, she told the minister, in full view of the public, that she wanted to pursue her further studies in Bhubaneswar. Impressed at his niece's desire to get a good education as well as her courage in publicly airing that desire, Majhi asked his staff to explore the possibilities of Murmu's admission in a Bhubaneswar school.

His staff immediately got to work and soon zeroed in on the Unit II Girls' High School in the capital city, which had a hostel for girls belonging to scheduled tribes (ST) and scheduled caste (SC) categories. The special hostel, now known as the Kuntala Kumari Sabat Hostel, had been set up by the Tribal and Rural Welfare (TRW) department (now christened the ST & SC Development, Minorities and Backward Classes department), a few years before Murmu moved to Bhubaneswar. There were two or three seats earmarked for ST and SC students from each of the thirteen (now thirty) districts in the state depending on the total population and the share of STs and SCs in a particular district. The names of students were recommended by the respective district administrations, based on which the department made the final selection.

To get admission in the hostel, one needed to produce a caste certificate to prove that she belonged to the ST (tribal) category, besides an income certificate. Getting these certificates issued was not easy those days—certainly not for her semi-literate father (he studied only up to Class III), blissfully ignorant of the ways of the world outside his village. Caste certificates were issued by the office of the collector and district magistrate located in Baripada, the district headquarters located 105 kilometres away from Uparbeda. But Murmu managed to get the all-important certificate through the good offices of the minister.

Murmu may not have faced much difficulty in procuring the caste certificate. But life in the new place was not easy for her and her ministerial connection did not help her overcome the difficulties she faced in Bhubaneswar. She had to keep all her girlie desires aside as Rs 10 was all her father could afford to send her every month by way of expenses. These days, virtually all expenses of tribal students, including boarding, lodging, attire, study materials, even bicycles and laptops, are taken care of by the government. But that was not the case in the late 1960s and early 1970s, when Murmu was in high school. The only facilities students could avail those days were two square meals a day, besides free boarding. Boarders, therefore, had to spend from their pockets for everything, from study materials to essential items like oil and soaps. With just Rs 10 a month, there was thus absolutely no scope for any indulgences for Murmu.

'In the four years that she spent in school, she did not visit the school canteen even once. When one of us offered to treat her with the stuff available in the canteen, she would politely decline the offer. Even at that young age, she valued self-esteem very much,' Suchitra Samal, her classmate in school told this author.

'She would sit in the back benches with other tribal girls. It is not as if we did not want to partake of the mouth-watering stuff gorged on by others. But we had to kill our desire since we simply did not have the money to buy the stuff,' corroborates Dangi Murmu, Murmu's fellow boarder and lifelong friend who also hails from Mayurbhanj, in an interview with this writer. Everyone in the hostel used to look forward to the two days in a week when non-vegetarian food was served by the mess.

Like most others in the hostel, Murmu had to make do with just one pair of dress, which she had to wash overnight every alternate day to wear the next morning. She would get up at 4 a.m., clean up her room and then join others in sweeping the hostel floor to get it ready for the morning prayers. Blessed as she was with a sweet voice, she would also lead the prayers.

She would rarely sit idle and always kept herself busy with something or the other when she was not studying. 'I was a little lazy in school and would often doze off. She would wake me up, saying, "Why are you sleeping? Let us go on a walk,"' Dangi says. 'While having food, we used to sit close to each other and competed to determine who finished first. Sometimes, she did. At other times, I did,' she says with a playful sparkle in her eyes.

Both Murmu and Dangi joined the National Cadet Corps (NCC) in school and took part in the drills and other activities with great enthusiasm. 'But it would remain a perennial regret for both of us that we could not represent our state at the Republic Day parade in New Delhi just because we could not afford the Rs 60 needed by way of expenses for participation in the event,' Dangi says ruefully.

The boarders had to take turns every month managing the hostel mess. The boarder incharge of the mess had to accompany the cook and the attendant to the market to buy grocery, vegetables and other stuff required for cooking, and maintain stocks. Another boarder played the role of a timekeeper, sounding the bell for the start of the study hour, lunch or dinner time, and so on. There was a lot else for the boarders to do. They tended to the garden, grew vegetables like brinjals, tomatoes, chillies and cabbage on the land inside the hostel premises, which partially took care of the vegetable requirements of the mess. They even had to learn and do stitching and embroidery. But there were no sewing machines; all the cutting, stitching and embroidery had to be done with bare hands. All this left very little time for recreation.

Everyone dreaded the hostel superintendent. A stern look from her would send shivers down the spines of boarders. The hostel rooms were so located that the superintendent could keep a watch on the boarders while sitting in her office room. Boarders were allowed to go home only once in a year, during the summer vacations.

'The rules in hostel were very strict and the punishment severe for any violations. On the rare occasions when we were allowed to go out, we were always accompanied by an attendant who kept a hawk eye on our movements and activities. We did not even have the freedom to look sideways and had to keep looking straight while we moved,' Murmu herself had said in an interview to Dr Samanta while reminiscing about those bygone days. The only indulgence the girls allowed themselves was to discard the school uniform and wear sarees on special occasions like a puja.

Given the restrictions on movement, the boarders knew precious little about the world lying beyond the school premises even though they stayed in the state capital. 'We were like frogs in the well,' Murmu would say years later about those days. Nor did anyone bother about life and career after school. Tuitions were unheard of in those times and students had to bank entirely on what they were taught in school while appearing in examinations. They lived in the present, happy with their life despite all the hardships. 'Murmu was the all-rounder among us. She excelled in sports, music, dance and drama. She would take part in all sporting activities like running, shotput and discus throw and would often win prizes in these events,' Dangi says. 'Memories of our hostel days came flooding into the mind as I watched Murmu take the oath of office and then deliver her first speech as President,' adds Dangi, who was specially invited by her old buddy for the swearing-in ceremony at Rashtrapati Bhavan on 25 July 2022.

As news of Murmu's nomination as the NDA's presidential candidate spread, impromptu celebrations broke out in her former school in Bhubaneswar. Sweets were distributed among students and teachers of the school. Inmates of the Kuntala Kumari Sabat Hostel, where she stayed, were particularly excited at the prospect of a former boarder becoming the President of India. Clasping each other's hands, they danced till they were thoroughly exhausted. Both the school and the hostel have undergone a sea change in the intervening years. The tiled roof has now been replaced by a concrete roof. The infrastructure and the ambience, too, have undergone radical changes. But what has not changed is the spirit that shaped the life of Murmu.

'Though I was not there at the time when she stayed here, I have heard from others that she was a role model as a student and had an excellent rapport with both her fellow students and teachers. We are extremely proud that an alumnus of the school and a former boarder of the hostel is going to become the President,' said Usha Munda, assistant superintendent of the hostel.

Unlike Munda, Smita Mohanty, a teacher in the school, had the privilege of meeting the would-be President. The occasion was the diamond jubilee of the school in 2019 where Murmu, then the Governor of Jharkhand, was a guest. 'She was extremely happy with the strides the school had taken and the progress it had made in the years since she passed out. It was a privilege to listen to her as she narrated her experience as a student and a boarder,' she reminisced about the meeting fours year ago while speaking to leading Odia TV news channel OTV.

After completing her high school education, Murmu went back to her village. She wanted to pursue higher studies. But given the poor state of communication those days, she did not get to know about the commencement of the admission process. By the time she did, the last date for admission had already passed. As a result, she lost a year after school. She spent the year doing household chores and teaching younger girls in village. But determined as she was to be a graduate, she took no chances the next year and duly took admission in the Ramadevi Women's College, the premier women's college in Bhubaneswar which now is a full-fledged university. However, since the hostel for ST and SC students in the college was not yet ready, she continued boarding in her old school hostel for some more time.

Her former classmates and contemporaries remember her as a quiet, disciplined girl who denied herself the ordinary pleasures that her batchmates indulged in. She was not exactly an outstanding student but was extremely attentive in classes, never participating in the pranks other students were up to. She would borrow books and notes from her seniors and ask them to help her out with a subject if she had a problem understanding something. 'She consulted me and other seniors on what subjects to choose for the undergraduate and graduate classes,' says Delha Soren, her senior in college, in an interview with this author.

There was great camaraderie among the boarders in the hostel, who came from similar sociocultural milieu. 'There were five girls in every room. If someone was busy with something when the dining bell was sounded, others would keep her meal ready. If it suddenly started raining, whoever was present would collect the dresses of everyone, not just her own, hung outside for drying,' shares Delha.

With the pittance she got as monthly allowance from her father, there was no scope for indulgences in college for Murmu. In her four years at Ramadevi, she did not go to the college canteen even once, rarely went to the market and watched just one movie, an Odia film called *Gapa Hele Bi Sata* at the now defunct Ravi Talkies. She would mostly hang out with girls from Mayurbhanj. But she would come into her own whenever there was a sports meet or a cultural function in the college. 'She excelled in sports and often ended up on the podium,' recalls retired Prof. Anima Kar, who taught her at Ramadevi, while talking to this writer. 'I remember because I used to do the running commentary,' she adds.

'She was most sought after whenever there was a cultural event in the college or the hostel because not only did she sing very well, she also played the percussion instruments to perfection,' remembers Gayamani Besra, her senior in college and a lifelong friend. 'During annual functions in the college, we would organize an adivasi dance item and sing and play the *tunda,* which is a tribal musical instrument. She was so good at what she did. Everybody appreciated her skills as a singer and musician. She was a happy-go-lucky girl but was always respectful towards seniors.' Besra is among those specially invited by Murmu for the swearing-in ceremony. She adds, 'She would invariably be part of the choir that sang the opening song at every cultural function in the college.'

Once, the girls of the hostel staged a play in which Murmu played the 'hero'. 'It was such a huge success that there was an invitation from a cultural group in Baripada, the headquarters of Murmu's home district of Mayurbhanj, to stage the drama there. Murmu and the troupe travelled to Baripada and performed the play there to thunderous applause,' recalls Delha.

Murmu was a quiet girl alright, but she was never shy of speaking up when she felt something wasn't fair. 'She never contested any election in college, not even for a class representative. But her leadership qualities were evident even in those early years. I remember an occasion when there was an issue about the quality of food served in the hostel. She led a delegation of students that met the principal and got the issue sorted,' says Surama Padhi, senior BJP leader and a former minister in the Odisha government who was her senior in college, in an interview with this author.

Beneath her shy exterior lay nerves of steel. Once, she was on her way to the hostel from the bus stand on a rickshaw with her senior Delha when they realized a boy was following them on a bicycle. Without panicking one bit, Murmu took out a bundle of twigs she had brought from home to be used as toothbrush (no one in the hostel used toothbrush in those days) and waved it at the street Romeo, who panicked and stopped following them.

Kanak Manjari Mishra, who taught her economics in college and was also the superintendent of the hostel where Murmu stayed, fondly remembers her former ward as a 'very good, obedient' girl. The two of them shared a very close relationship, particularly because Murmu was the manager of the college mess. 'Since my residence was in the college premises, she and some of her friends would often come to my place and spend time with me. There was a wall hanging in my drawing room which had several moral lessons written on it. She copied them on her notebook. I, too, used to visit the hostel in the evenings and spend time with the boarders. Not that I wanted to keep an eye on them. They were all nice girls who never strayed out of line. So, there never was a need to discipline them. On special occasions, I and the hostel matron Brajeswari Mishra used to sponsor some eatables for the boarders to make them feel good,' Mishra shares while speaking to this writer.

Murmu was equally fond of her former superintendent and matron. 'I would never forget the love and affection of Brajeswari Mishra, matron of my hostel. Economics teacher Kanak Manjari Mishra was my favourite. As I was in charge of the hostel mess management, I was very close to her,' she wrote about her former teachers in a souvenir brought out by the

Old Students' Association to mark the first convocation of Rama Devi Women's University in 2017. Murmu, who was the Governor of Jharkhand at the time, was the chief guest on the occasion.

In a fitting tribute to an illustrious alumnus, Murmu's alma mater conferred an honorary doctorate on her at the convocation. It was a rare occasion when one Governor (the Governor of Odisha Prof. Ganeshi Lal) conferred a degree on another Governor (Murmu).

A government job was all that her contemporaries in college looked forward to and Murmu was no exception. She prepared diligently for competitive examinations and underwent mock tests conducted by her seniors. Fortunately for her, there was a special recruitment drive launched by the state government for STs. Murmu promptly applied for it and got a job as a junior assistant in the Irrigation department of the state government even before the results of her bachelor's degree examination were out. The year was 1979.

By then, her senior Delha, with whom she had developed a very intimate relationship, had got a job in the Accountant General (AG) office in Bhubaneswar and had been allotted a quarters in the AG Colony in Unit IV. Delha was sharing the house with Gayamani Besra, another senior of Murmu. Both were happy to invite Murmu to stay with them once the latter got a job in the state secretariat which, incidentally, was next to the AG office.

With money in hand, life became just a little easier for the three Mayurbhanj girls. Murmu and Delha would walk to their respective offices, not very far from the place where they stayed, together in the morning. On their way back, they would go to the Unit IV market to buy vegetables and anything else needed in the kitchen. The three of them—Gayamani, Delha and Murmu—would share not just the cooking responsibilities, but also their sarees. 'Murmu was always an early riser. She would wake up at 4 a.m. and finish half the cooking by the time we were up,' recalls Delha.

It was Delha who introduced Murmu to her future husband Shyam Charan Murmu. Shyam used to work in the Divisional Accountant office in Puri, a unit of the AG office, at the time and would often come to the head office in Bhubaneswar on work. It was during one such trip that he met Murmu, who was with Delha, for the first time. Murmu started making enquiries with Delha about Murmu. After a couple of meetings, Shyam asked Delha, 'I want to propose to Droupadi. What do you think?' 'Go right ahead,' said Delha.

After marriage, Murmu left the AG Colony quarters and started living with her husband at a rented accommodation in the Shastri Nagar area in Bhubaneswar. Shyam would commute to Puri, a distance of 55 kilometres, daily while Murmu would work in Bhubaneswar.

A year after their marriage, the couple were blessed with their first child, a daughter, whom they named 'Bada Mama'.

# 6

# Back to Base

With no one to look after her daughter once she left for office, life in Bhubaneswar was not easy for Murmu, especially after she became a mother. Things grew even more difficult for her after her husband got a job as an officer in a public-sector bank. There was pressure on her from her in-laws to come over and stay with her husband. But the proverbial last straw on the camel's back was when her daughter, aged just three, died of pneumonia in 1983.

Quitting a secure, reasonably well-paid government job was not an easy decision to take for someone who had spent her life in penury till then. But circumstances forced her to take the call. Without resigning from her job, she shifted base to stay with her husband, who was posted in the neighbouring state of Jharkhand at the time.

In the years that followed, she kept shuttling between Pahadpur, her in-laws' place, her husband's place of posting and Rairangpur town. Since her husband was staying away, she looked after farming activities on their family land, often joining the labourers to keep them motivated. Once her husband got posted in Rairangpur, she rented a house in town. Sometime in the early 1990s, her husband bought a house in Rairangpur from a colleague in the bank after availing of a loan. The house, located in the Mahuldiha area of the town, underwent some expansion and modification in the years that followed.

During this period, she had three more children; two sons and a daughter. Raising them kept her engaged full time, leaving her with very little time for anything else. However, once the children grew up and started going to school, she didn't have much to do at home during daytime. Her restless spirit craved for something meaningful to keep her engaged.

Nearly a decade after she shifted based to Rairangpur, Murmu got an offer to teach at the Sri Aurobindo Integral Education and Research Center. Given her love for education, she was delighted at this offer. But she had one condition; she would not accept any remuneration for her services. She made it clear to the school management that she was accepting the offer only for her love of education and, of course, her love for children. In any case, her husband's salary as a bank officer was enough to take care of the family expenses. The decision to work gratis was an early indication of Murmu's spirit of selfless public service.

Going by the accounts of her former colleagues and students about her days at the school, Murmu was a very popular teacher. She loved her students, who reciprocated in equal measure. She was always friendly with them and never got angry with or punished anyone during the three years, from 1994 to 1997, she spent there.

'She had a unique way of keeping the children interested and engaged. She would always come with a bundle of chocolates and keep them on the table before starting her class. She would ask questions and would hand over a chocolate to whoever gave the correct answer,' says Abhishek Das, one of her former students.

Another great quality about Murmu the teacher that emerges after talking to her ex-students is that she had no favourites and treated everyone equally, whether a student was bright or a backbencher. 'She would narrate incidents from the lives of great people in class and ask us to follow their examples,' says Rajesh Behera, another of her former students, adding, 'Now, we have the privilege of citing *her* example.'

'She was a very strong-willed woman and would never rest till she finished the task given to her. Though we never imagined that she would one day go on to become the President of the country, we did know that she would rise high in life,' says Indira Otta, a teacher in the school and a former colleague of Murmu.

Dillip Kumar Giri, the school caretaker, is among the few who were there when Murmu taught in the school. Reminiscing about those days, he told this author, 'She treated me like a younger brother and I used to address her as "Didi". She knew my wife and children too. When she visited the school in connection with the 150th birth anniversary celebrations of Sri Aurobindo last year [15 August 2022], she took time off to ask me about their well-being.'

Murmu herself has never forgotten her three-year stint as a teacher in the school and the role it played in shaping her life even after 'rising high'. In interviews she has given to media outlets, she has always made it a point to mention the fulfilling time she spent there and the wonderful relationship she enjoyed with her students. 'She did not take even a second to say "yes" when we invited her to be the chief guest at the ceremony to launch the year-long celebration of the 150th birth anniversary of Sri Aurobindo. She spent considerable time here speaking to the students and teachers and sharing memories of her time in the school,' says Pramila Swain, the headmistress of the school, while speaking to this writer.

When this author reached the school three days after Murmu was sworn in as President, the first thing that struck him was a large billboard outside the school gate hailing the newly anointed constitutional head. 'We are proud of our President Madam Murmu, ex teacher of our school. Our Regards, Congratulations & Best Wishes to Madam,' read the billboard. Inside, a framed picture of Murmu with her colleagues had pride of place on the walls of the school office.

Rabindra Patnaik, the head of the school management committee, is a proud man today. 'It's a matter of great pride for all of us that the first citizen of India was once a teacher at this school. It is because of her that our school is now known throughout the country. We have no doubt that her elevation to the highest constitutional post would inspire us to work harder and make this school the No. 1 Aurobindo school in the country,' he says.

Even after she started teaching in the school, Murmu still had some time on her hands. Given the kind of person she is, she started participating in various social activities in Rairangpur and nearby areas. This enlarged her circle of friends and acquaintances.

She went out of her way to help people in distress. Her philanthropic work soon got noticed and she acquired a reputation as a selfless do-gooder. But there was no sign yet of the sharp turn her life was set to take soon.

# 7

# Political Plunge

Politics was the last thing on Murmu's mind till she worked as a teacher at the Sri Aurobindo school. But perhaps there was an air of inevitability about the fact that she did, in the end, take the political plunge. For one thing, she is the descendant of a family of *sardar*s (village chieftains), an honorific given to her forefathers by the then rulers of Mayurbhanj for their services to the kingdom in the nineteenth century.[1] 'Droupadi's father and grandfather were both village *pradhan*s (chiefs) and were highly respected in the community even though the family had fallen on bad times financially by the time she was born,' her former teacher Basudev Behera told this author.

For another, the soil of Uparbeda, Murmu's native village, had proved particularly fertile for politics to grow in the post-Independence era. It is a measure of the fertility of the soil that three out of the thirteen MLAs that the Rairangpur (ST) constituency has elected since the first elections in free India in 1952, besides one Lok Sabha MP, have been from Uparbeda. The first of them was Kartik Chandra Majhi, a member of Murmu's extended family, who was elected to the Odisha Assembly on a Swatantra Party ticket way back in 1967. Though he was a first-time MLA, Majhi was made a minister and held several ministerial portfolios, including Home and Finance, in the Maharaja R.N. Singhdeo government between 1967 and 1971. The next in line was Bhabendra Nath Majhi, an engineer who left his cushy job at Central Coalfields Limited to fight—and win—the 1985 Assembly elections on a Congress ticket. Unfortunately, however, he passed away within a year of being elected to the Assembly. In the mid-1990s, Salkhan Murmu, who was employed with Tata Steel in Jamshedpur, was persuaded by BJP leaders to contest the Lok Sabha elections as a party candidate. He lost his first election in 1996, but then went on to win twice in succession after that—in 1998 and 1999. And no prizes for guessing who the third person to represent the Rairangpur constituency in the Odisha Assembly was!

There was thus no dearth of inspiration, either in the family or in the village, for Murmu to join politics. But till 1997, she had not contemplated, even in passing, a career in politics. She was happy with her life as a teacher and loved spending time with children. When she was first approached by local BJP leaders to join the party and fight the municipal election from Ward No. 2 in Rairangpur in 1997, she was not at all keen. Rajkishore Das, the foremost BJP leader in the area who was seeking a second successive term as the chairperson of the Rairangur Notified Area Council (NAC), had zeroed in on Murmu after getting positive feedback about her from others. By then, Murmu had earned a reputation not only as a very popular teacher but also as a social worker of sorts with her active involvement in various philanthropic activities. She fitted the bill perfectly since Ward No. 2 was reserved for a woman belonging to the ST category.

'I was very impressed with whatever I heard about Murmu ji from friends and party colleagues. Here was a woman from a humble background in a nondescript tribal village, who had dared to dream. She had left her village and gone to Bhubaneswar to pursue higher education at a time when it was difficult even for boys in the area to do so. The BJP did not have a good base in the area at the time. The Congress and the JMM held sway there. We thought she would be a good investment for the future since she was a tribal—and that too a Santhal, who constitute a majority in the area—and a woman. So, we initiated efforts to rope her into the party fold and field her in the upcoming municipal elections,' says Das, whom Murmu considers her mentor and political 'guru', while talking to this author.

Das, now the BJD MLA from the Morada Assembly constituency in Mayurbhanj (he switched over to the ruling party on the eve of the 2019 elections), first sent feelers to Murmu through a fellow teacher, the late Dibakar Mohanta. But Murmu was non-committal. BJP emissaries then met Murmu's husband and requested him to persuade her. But Murmu was still undecided. The major reason for her reservation, as she herself said in an interview later, was the fact that her children were very young at the time. 'I thought politics would demand full-time involvement for which I was not prepared at the time. Besides, the politics that I had seen from afar was not a very comfortable prospect for someone, especially a woman, with a family to look after,' she had told her interviewer, Dr Samanta.

But the emissaries were insistent. 'You don't have to go outside. After all, you are not contesting an election for the Assembly or Parliament. We are there to help you at every step. All you need to do is to take out some time to look after the affairs of your ward, which has no more than 1500–2000 people,' they reasoned with her. But Murmu remained sceptical.

She was still weighing the pros and cons of agreeing to the proposal when senior BJP leader and former minister Manmohan Samal, the then state general secretary of the party in charge of four districts, including Mayurbhanj, met her at her residence in the company of Rajkishore Das. 'I told her, "You are already engaged in social work and politics would provide you a much bigger platform to do what you are doing. If you agree to join the BJP, work diligently and be patient, then the sky is the limit for you,"' Samal, who is now in his third term as president of the BJP state unit, told this author. His words were to prove prophetic nearly a quarter of a century later.

The sustained efforts by BJP leaders finally bore fruit. Murmu relented and agreed to join the party and fight the election. Nigamananda Patnaik, a long-time Sangh worker in the town, got her to sign the customary membership form to mark her entry into the party. He, along with Rajkishore Das and Jugal Rout, was part of the team that held talks with Murmu. Before the BJP, the Congress and the JMM, which were the two major parties in the region at the time, too had made efforts to win her over to their side. That she chose the fledgling BJP over them in the end can be attributed more to the perseverance and persuasive powers of the crack team that worked on her rather than any love for the party or its worldview. Till that point, there was nothing that even remotely suggested that she subscribed to the ideology of the saffron party—or any party, for that matter. In any case, the BJP was not a force to reckon with in the region where the Congress, the JMM and the Janata Dal (the precursor of the BJD) were the major political players.

In wooing Murmu, the BJP was trying to break the stranglehold of the JMM among the Santhals in the area, who numbered nearly three lakh in the district. For the Santhals of the area, Shibu Soren, the JMM founder, was God. Thousands of people assembled at every meeting addressed by him. Sudam Marandi, now a senior leader of the ruling BJD and a former minister, was the rising star of the outfit that sought the inclusion of three northern districts in Odisha, including Mayurbhanj, with the state of Jharkhand that it was demanding.

The roping in of Salkhan Murmu into the fold earlier was part of the same BJP strategy. While the move had not paid immediate dividends—Salkhan lost the 1996 Lok Sabha elections—subsequent developments vindicated the soundness of the strategy as he went on to win the Lok Sabha polls from the Mayurbhanj constituency in both 1998 and 1999. The BJP persisted with the strategy in the years that followed and emerged as a powerful political entity, winning six Assembly seats in the district along with the Mayurbhanj Lok Sabha seat in the 2019 elections. The BJP MP from the Lok Sabha constituency is now the minister of state for Tribal Affairs and Jal Shakti (Water Resources) in the Modi government. The creation of the Tribal Affairs ministry by the Vajpayee government in 1999 was also part of the BJP's strategy to increase its footprint in the tribal heartland across the country.

Meanwhile, Murmu, who had no previous experience of politics, sailed through her first election, winning from Ward No. 2 by a comfortable margin without straining a sinew. In a move to woo the numerically significant Santhals of the region, she was also appointed the vice chairperson of NAC, though she was a first-timer and a complete greenhorn in politics.

Murmu was given charge of sanitation in the town. Though a complete novice, she brought to her job the sincerity, freshness of approach and enthusiasm that is, more often than not, the hallmark of a newcomer. Curious people watched bemused as she personally supervised the clearing of garbage and cleaning of clogged drains in the town. She would roam the streets in a Maruti 800 her husband had bought to identify areas that needed intervention and would stand there, umbrella in hand—in sun and rain—passing instructions to the workers at work. Years before PM Modi launched it at a national level, Murmu had initiated her own Swachhata Abhijan (cleanliness campaign) at the local level. The people of Rairangpur, who had never seen anything of the sort before, were suitably impressed. In due course, her reputation as a committed do-gooder travelled beyond the municipal limits of Rairangpur.

Rajkishore Das, widely credited with spotting the potential in Murmu and mentoring her through her early years in politics, says that there were two qualities that marked her out as someone special. 'The first was her calm and cool demeanour. She had a disarming smile that could charm even enemies. I have never seen her lose her temper, no matter how grave the provocation is. Winning friends and influencing people came naturally to her. The second was her complete dedication to the job at hand,' he says.

It was this dedication that made her three-year stint as councillor and vice chairperson of the NAC a highly productive period. The BJP didn't have to look beyond her when it fought the 2000 Assembly elections in alliance with the BJD. Apart from the Rairangpur NAC, the Rairangpur Assembly constituency comprised two blocks—Kusumi and Jamda—at the time. (After delimitation, the former is now part of the Jashipur Assembly seat). Both Uparbeda and Pahadpur came under Kusumi block. The nomination of Murmu from Rairangpur thus made eminent political sense.

It was, however, not as if there were no other aspirants in the party for a ticket to contest the polls from Rairangpur. Nandalal Soren, a dedicated BJP worker, was a strong contender and had the right credentials for the ticket. But what apparently clinched the issue in favour of Murmu in the end was that she was a woman. Manmohan Samal says the BJP, which did not have many women in its fold, was making a conscious effort to induct and groom women at the time. And an educated Santhal woman like Murmu was a godsend for the party trying to get a foothold in a playing arena dominated by the Congress, the JMM and the Janata Dal. Peeved at being denied the party ticket, Soren contested the election as an independent candidate but lost. After winning the election, Murmu won him over by giving him the importance he deserved as a long-time worker of the party.

In Laxman Majhi of the Congress, Murmu had a formidable opponent since Majhi was the sitting MLA and the Congress was in power in the state. She also had to contend with the JMM, which had a significant presence in the region. But in the end, it was the rookie politician with no previous experience of fighting an Assembly election who came up trumps against an array of formidable opponents. Her stint as the vice chairperson of the Rairangpur NAC certainly helped, as did the fact that the Kusumi block constituted a significant part of the constituency.

What also worked in her favour was the fact that she had a band of dedicated party workers willing to work tirelessly for her. Among her earliest associates in the area was Dambarudhar Mohanta, the then sarpanch of Uparbeda panchayat. 'I had known her since her childhood. She was a good student and was always keen to come to the aid of others. She had already proved her mettle as a councillor and vice chairperson of the Rairangpur NAC. During discussions in party forums, I strongly pitched for her. Her name was already being discussed as a prospective candidate from the constituency when she came to me and said, "Dambaru Bhai, I would contest, only if you assure me of your support." I assured her I will,' Mohanta told this author in an interview.

Lack of funds failed to curb the enthusiasm of BJP workers determined to break the stranglehold of the JMM and the Congress and spread the party's footprint in the area. 'What we got from the party by way of election expenses was a pittance. We did not even have money to buy petrol for our bikes. Most of us travelled on bicycles. I was the only one who was given a Rajdoot bike and Rs 100, which took care of the fuel expenses for close to three days. We slept in the party office and ate whatever food we got from our supporters in the town. During campaigning, we managed with whatever our supporters fed us. I remember one occasion when we went without food all day during hectic campaigning. As we were returning in the evening, a member of the group said he was terribly hungry and couldn't take it any more.

I searched my pocket and found that 90 paise was all I had. I was almost in tears at the sheer helplessness of not being able to feed my team. Seeing our plight, the owner of a roadside eatery offered us some *gulgula*, a flour-based local eatable. But we did not allow the lack of funds to affect the campaigning. We more than made up for what we lacked in terms of money with our zeal and enthusiasm,' says Hari Prasad Sahu, a long-time associate of Murmu and a key BJP organizer in the area.

While the party workers did the hard work, it was a fun trip for others in Murmu's entourage. 'I never felt we were in the serious business of election campaigning. It was more like a picnic for me. We would pick berries and other fruits and eat them with some salt offered by villagers,' says Saraswati Tudu, Murmu's aunt who was a college student at the time, while speaking to this author. Saraswati, who was the athletics champion in college, mobilized her fellow students who, in turn, influenced their parents to vote for Murmu. 'We were a trio. Apart from Droupadi and me, there was Poma, a cousin of Droupadi, who knew a lot of people in the area. Hence, we never faced any problem while campaigning,' says Saraswati, who is nearly twenty years younger than Murmu.

Murmu herself would move from village to village, door to door, interacting with the people and listening to their problems. The workers would reach the village before Murmu, speak to the village head and assemble the people when she arrived. The Santhal kinship ties came in handy for Murmu during the campaign. Since word about her good work as the NAC vice chairperson had spread in the nearby areas, she was not exactly a stranger for the people of her constituency. Her earnest personal approach during campaigning was a refreshing change for the people long used to watching politicians breeze through villages on a vehicle, waving to the people and flashing a practised plastic smile. Murmu came as a breath of fresh air. The people, who were disillusioned with the unfulfilled promises made by previous MLAs, including the incumbent Laxman Majhi, welcomed the change. What also helped was the support of the BJD workers, its alliance partner.

When the votes were counted, it emerged that the 'greenhorn' had bested all the seasoned politicians to win the seat by a margin of 4568 votes; not exactly a landslide, but creditable nonetheless since she was making her debut in an Assembly election and her party at the time was far from the powerful force that it is today. Murmu had done the unthinkable by winning from a seat where the BJP was a non-entity till then. And the party was suitably impressed. She was made a minister—with independent charge, mind you—even though she was a first-time MLA. This was the second time in three years that Murmu got the big prize after winning her first election; the first being when she was made the vice chairperson of the Rairangpur NAC after winning her first election as a councillor.

'Rajkishore Das was insistent that she be made a minister. In any case, there were not too many among those elected on BJP ticket who had won more than once. Arabinda Dhali from Malkangiri was the only one who had won thrice—in 1992 (by-election), 1995 and then in 2000. There were only three others—K.V. Singh Deo from Patnagarh, Pradeep Nayak from Bhawanipatna and Samir Dey from Cuttack—who had won two successive elections in 1995 and 2000. So, it was not a problem nominating Murmu for a ministerial berth,' says Manmohan Samal, who was the state unit president of the BJP at the time.

As per the terms agreed upon by the alliance partners—BJD and BJP—both parties were allocated a certain number of ministerial positions in a ratio of 4:3, just as in the case of MLA seats (84:63). Even the portfolios were allocated on a party basis. As per the formula worked out between the two parties, the BJP state unit was to recommend the names of its MLAs for ministerial positions. 'We discussed the issue in our core committee meeting and included Murmu ji's name among those recommended for places in the council of ministers. Since she was a first-timer, we had initially recommended her name as minister of state for the relatively less challenging department of Planning and Coordination. We had even sent the list of ministers with their prospective portfolios from our party to CM Naveen Patnaik. But after further deliberations following a demand from the Mayurbhanj unit that she be considered for a more important portfolio, there was a last-minute change and her name was recommended as minister of state (independent charge) for Commerce and Transport. The list sent to the CM earlier was withdrawn and a fresh list with the change in Murmu's portfolio sent just hours before the swearing-in ceremony,' says Samal.

Just as she had done after becoming the vice chairperson of the Rairangpur NAC on winning her first election, Murmu brought to her job a rare zeal and enthusiasm, which more than made up for her lack of administrative experience. She worked hard and diligently to understand and master the nuances and intricacies of her new role as minister. She had always been a very meticulous person, who believed in doing her homework before taking a decision. The fact that she was also a patient listener certainly helped. Senior BJD leader Debi Prasad Mishra, her ministerial colleague at the time, says she put her heart and soul into anything she took up. 'As a first-timer, it was understandable that she was not very proactive at meetings of the council of ministers. But she did participate in the deliberations and was not shy of speaking her mind if she felt strongly about a certain issue,' he says.

In discharging her ministerial responsibilities, she was helped in no small measure by Bijay Nayak, who was appointed her private secretary. Nayak, during his student days, had been closely associated with the Akhil Bharatiya Vidyarthi Parishad, the students' wing of the BJP, and had become the president of the students' union in Utkal University, the premier university in Odisha. He is also an eminent littérateur, who has been the editor of *Kahani*, a literary magazine, for two decades.

Going by the accounts of those who saw up close the Murmu–Bijay duo work in tandem, he was a very efficient and diligent officer who guided the first time MLA and minister the right way. Nayak remained her private secretary even when she was made the minister of state for Fisheries and Animal Husbandry during a reshuffle of the council of ministers after two years. Their relationship, based on mutual trust and respect, has stood the test of time even though Murmu never became a minister ever again after her first tenure. It's a measure of the enduring relationship between the two that Nayak was appointed the additional press secretary at Rashtrapati Bhavan after Murmu became the President. She was keen to have Nayak as her private secretary even when she was Governor of Jharkhand and had personally requested the Odisha CM to spare him. But for reasons that can only be speculated on, her request was not granted.

With able handholding by Nayak, Murmu was quick to size up her ministerial responsibilities. She realized that unlike many other departments, hers was essentially a revenue-generating department and not a development or welfare portfolio. Hence, she concentrated on efforts to plug leakages and increase revenue generation by the department. One of the major sources of earning for the department were the twenty-three inter-state check gates in the state where most of the pilferage took place. Through her trusted officers, she kept a hawk eye on the collections. She also started a system of quarterly reviews, which kept her officers on their toes. Over a period of time, the leakages were plugged and revenue generation saw a quantum jump over previous years. Chief Minister Naveen Patnaik was mighty impressed with her performance.

The other major area of Murmu's intervention as a minister, however, was focus on public convenience rather than revenue generation. Though Odisha had thirty districts, there were only fifteen Regional Transport Offices (RTOs) in the state at the time: one each for the thirteen districts that were split into thirty in 1992 during the reign of Biju Patnaik, Naveen Patnaik's father, plus one each in Bhubaneswar, the capital city, and Rourkela, the steel city. This meant that people of as many as seventeen districts had to go to the RTO office in a neighbouring district to get their vehicles registered, their driving licences issued or renewed, and sundry other work. Even within a district, people in some of the larger districts had to commute long distances to reach the RTO, usually located in the district headquarters. A case in point was Murmu's home district of Mayurbhanj, where the people of Rairangpur had to travel to Baripada, the district headquarters located over 100 kilometres away. For people living in areas north of Rairangpur, like Jashipur and Tiring, the distance was even more. This posed great inconvenience to the people. Realizing the problem, Murmu initiated a move to open RTOs in all thirty districts and Additional Regional Transport Offices (ARTOs) in places far off from the nearest RTO within a district. The move was a huge relief for the people, who were saved the trouble of commuting long distances and could now get all their RTO-related work done close to their homes.

Her former aides say she was quick to study and clear files. 'Though she was a first-timer both as MLA and minister, she did not allow IAS officers to call the shots and fiercely guarded her turf as minister while taking a call on an issue. She would diligently read the file notings before taking a decision. And once she made up her mind, she would never change it no matter what the possible consequences were,' says one of them, requesting anonymity.

Murmu displayed the same enthusiasm and dedication in her job even when she was moved from the Commerce and Transport department and given the Fisheries and Animal Husbandry portfolio. Under her stewardship, the department opened several fishing harbours along the vast coastline of the state to boost fish production. She also framed a reservoir policy to facilitate intensive fishing. Realizing that there were too few livestock inspectors (LIs) to look after activities like poultry and goatery, she took the initiative to appoint more LIs to increase the livestock population and sanctioned the required funds for construction of quarters for them.

One of her major achievements during her stint as minister, however, had nothing to do with her ministerial responsibilities. It was a cause dear to her heart: the recognition and popularization of Santhali language, the language spoken by the Santhals. With a population of about six million, the Santhals constitute the third-biggest scheduled tribe (ST) in India, after the Bhils and Gonds. Santhali, however, is spoken not just by Santhals but also by the Ho and Mundari tribes. Part of the Munda sub-family of the Austroasiatic language, Santhali is spoken by around seven million people across the Indian states of Odisha, West Bengal, Tripura, Mizoram, Jharkhand and Bihar, besides parts of Bangladesh, Bhutan and Nepal. It is the third most spoken Austroasiatic language after Vietnamese and Khmer.

Unfortunately, however, Santhali did not get due recognition despite the vast number of people who spoke the language in India and its neighbourhood, largely because it did not have a script. European researchers and missionaries used the Bengali, Odia or Roman script to document the Santhali language in the nineteenth century. But they could not really capture the unique phonetics of Santhali, which remained a largely spoken language till Pandit Raghunath Murmu, a native of Mayurbhanj and a tribal scholar, developed the Ol Chiki script in 1925. Even Pandit Murmu wrote his early books in the Odia script before he developed the Ol Chiki script. But once he did, he wrote a large number of books in Santhali using his Ol Chiki script and toured extensively in Odisha, Bengal and Bihar to popularize his newly developed script. He also pleaded with the state and the central governments to accord recognition to Santhali.

Despite Pandit Murmu's best efforts, however, the Santhali language did not get what it deserved, either among the linguists or in the Constitution. Convinced about the antiquity and richness of the language, Murmu took it upon herself to get it its rightful place. She talked to CM Naveen Patnaik numerous times and convinced him about the need to give due recognition to the language. As a member of the Tribal Advisory Council (TAC) of the state government, she got a resolution passed at a council meeting seeking the inclusion of the Santhali language in the Eighth Schedule of the Constitution and had it submitted to the Union Home department for a decision.

Fortunately for Murmu—and for the language she was championing—Justice Ranganath Misra, a retired Chief Justice of India (CJI) and a native of Odisha, was the head of the Union Home ministry's panel on languages at the time. He responded positively to the resolution sent by the state government and placed it with the Home minister with a strong recommendation. But despite the favourable response of Justice Misra, Murmu felt the matter needed attention at the highest level of the Union government and decided to meet PM Vajpayee to plead the case of Santhali. She approached M. Kharavela Swain, the three-time BJP MP from the Balasore constituency, to facilitate a meeting with Vajpayee. 'Thanks to Kharavela Bhai, we got an appointment with the PM in just ten minutes,' Murmu said in an interview to Dr Samanta much later.

'I knew it won't be easy to meet Vajpayee ji at the PMO. It's much easier to get an audience with him in the Parliament House. So, I took Murmu ji with me to Parliament, which was in session at the time. I met the PM's private secretary and requested him to arrange a meeting with Vajpayee ji. The call came within a few minutes,' Swain told this writer.

Murmu, in the company of Swain and her private secretary Bijay Nayak, met PM Vajpayee and presented him a book titled *Santhali: The Base of World Languages* by Parimal Chandra Mitra. 'Vajpayee ji flipped through the book and muttered, "Achcha [Good]." He was very impressed when I told him that unlike most Indian languages, Santhali has no "matras" [vowel diacritic]. He assured me that he would ensure its inclusion in the Eighth Schedule,' Murmu told her interviewer. True to his words, Santhali did get constitutional recognition with its inclusion in the Eighth Schedule in about six months' time. And Murmu played a historical role in this by taking what Pandit Raghunath Murmu had started before Independence to its logical conclusion. She got a pat on the back from CM Patnaik on the floor of the House for the role she had played in the constitutional recognition of Santhali. She was actively involved in the publication of an eight-page monthly magazine *Fagun* in Santhali language written in the Santhali language and Ol Chiki script. It was launched in 2003 when she was a minister.

Her love for Ol Chiki and her commitment to earning the rightful place for it, however, predates her becoming a minister and even her entry into politics. Speaking to this writer, Ramachandra Murmu, a retired Reserve Bank of India (RBI) officer who knows her closely since her college days, says even as a student, she would take part in various conferences organized for popularization of the Santhali language and the Ol Chiki script. 'Santhals from neighbouring states like West Bengal and Bihar used to take part in such conferences and share their thoughts and ideas on how to win recognition for the script,' he adds.

Having earned for Santhali a place in the Eighth Schedule of the Constitution, Murmu turned her attention to *Chandamama*, the now defunct but then extremely popular multilingual monthly children's magazine, which was already being published in Odia as *Janha Mamu*, besides twelve other languages. She wrote to the publishers, impressing upon them the need to have a Santhali version of the magazine since the language was spoken by millions of people. The publishers accepted her request and *Chandamama* was duly published in Santhali.

It was, however, not just the Santhali language or the Ol Chiki script that drew her attention. She went out of her way to take up any cause that had a bearing on the tribals. As a minister, she did everything she could to help the Adivasi Social, Economic and Cultural Association (ASECA), an organization working to protect and uphold the interests of tribals of all hues. She herself was a member of the organization.

Unlike most others, her demeanour did not change one bit after becoming a minister. There was no ministerial air about her. She remained the same humble, unassuming person she always was. 'Her greatest strength was her simplicity and humility. Her behaviour towards people never changed; not when she became a minister, not when she became a Governor, not even after she was named as the presidential candidate. The morning after her name was announced as the NDA's presidential nominee, I called her on phone. She greeted me with "Bhai, Namaskar. Jai Marang Buru [Santhali God]," just as she has always done,' says senior BJD leader and Murmu's erstwhile ministerial colleague Debi Prasad Mishra. 'She would never badmouth anyone, whether in her party or in the Opposition,' he adds while speaking to this writer.

Murmu's lifelong friend Gayamani Besra recalls an incident that showed that the trappings of power had failed to change her. 'Once, when she was a minister, she was in Rourkela, where I was posted at the time, to attend a Santhali convention. We wanted to meet her but were not too sure if we could get her attention. But the moment she saw us, she greeted us, joining her hands in a namaste,' she told this author.

Delha Soren, another lifelong friend, recollects a civic felicitation organized for Murmu at the IDCOL auditorium in Bhubaneswar soon after she became minister. 'I was seated in the first row. She was on the stage. The moment she saw me, she came down to greet me. It was such a touching gesture,' Soren told this author.

Power for her was not an end in itself but an opportunity to expand the scope of the social work she was already doing before entering politics. She never gave anyone a false assurance and always went out of her way to help people. She was perhaps the most accessible member of the council of ministers. The doors of her residence were always open for everyone. 'Anyone who came from Rairangpur, whether a common man or someone from a rival party, was given a warm welcome at her residence. The staff there were under strict instructions to provide food and accommodation to people from her area and to look after their comfort and well-being while they stayed there. There was a rest shed inside her residence where you would invariably find someone or the other from Rairangpur staying,' says Debashish Rout, a youth from Rairangpur town, who stayed with her for two years while pursuing his master's at Utkal University.

There is an endearing human side to Murmu's persona which wins over anyone who comes in contact with her. Debashish, the son of a family friend of Murmu, was staying in the university hostel. But when Murmu came to know about it, she was very upset. 'Why should you stay in a hostel when I am there? Get your luggage and move into my quarters by the end of the day,' she told him. 'During the two years I stayed with her, she treated me like a son, ensuring my well-being and taking on the role of a perfect guardian. While the others in the family had their meals on the dining table, she would always have her dinner sitting with me on the floor. One day, she came to my room and found a part of the mosquito net torn. She asked me why I had not told her about it earlier. When I returned in the evening after classes, I was pleasantly surprised to find that a new mosquito net had replaced the old one,' says a grateful Debashish.

Stories of the help she offered to people as a minister are well-known. Dillip Kumar Giri, the caretaker of the school where Murmu taught before entering politics, is among the countless people who received her benevolent support while she was a minister. 'My sister was suffering from cancer. When she came to know about it, she took the initiative and got an amount of Rs 50,000 sanctioned from the Chief Minister's Relief Fund (CMRF) for her treatment. It's another matter that she did not survive,' he recalls in an interview with this author.

One does not have to be close to Murmu to receive her benevolence. She went out of her way to help even those she did not know personally. 'There was this colleague of mine who had got some work in the Transport department. He had apparently heard that I knew Droupadi well and requested me to approach the minister on his behalf to get the work done. But I was not too keen to use our personal relationship to get a favour. So, I told him that we were just acquaintances and our relationship was not of the kind where I could approach her to get something done. Unknown to me, the colleague met the minister and got his work done,' recalls Gayamani Besra, Murmu's lifelong friend.

There was something special about Murmu that the discerning did not miss even when she was a relative greenhorn in politics. It was clear to them that she was cut out for bigger things. Bhrugu Baxipatra, the general secretary of the Odisha unit of BJP, recalls an anecdote from 2000 narrated to him by his late father, eminent socialist leader and former minister Harishchandra Baxipatra. 'A couple of months before his death, my father, who was the President of Utkal Sammilani, an organization working for the protection and advancement of Odia language and culture, at the time, had attended a function where Murmu ji was a guest. She had just become an MLA—and a minister—for the first time. But her speech at the function had obviously impressed my father very much. On coming home, he told me, "Her knowledge and erudition were truly remarkable. Mark my words, she would go far."' And far she did go, though twenty-two years later.

While discharging her ministerial duties, however, Murmu did not forget her responsibilities as an MLA. She frequently toured her constituency, patiently hearing out the people's problems and grievances and trying to address them using her new-found power to get issues sorted out: a handpump installed here, electricity connection provided there, and so on. It was during this period that a bridge was constructed on the river Kahnu, which made it possible for vehicles to reach Uparbeda and the area beyond. The problem of flooding of the main thoroughfare in the village in the monsoons was sorted out with diversion of the stream that caused the flooding.

But it was not just her own village that received her attention. She did the best she could to solve the problems of every village in her constituency. 'She was fair to everyone and never discriminated against any village or community when it came to providing succour. She would take copious notes while talking to people during her numerous visits to her constituency—jotting down individual and community problems separately in her diary. She would then decide which of them had to be pursued with the block office, which one with the Integrated Tribal Development Agency (ITDA), the Irrigation department or the electricity department. Most importantly, she would follow up on the work diligently. This way, she was able to fulfil most of the promises she made to people,' says Dambarudhar Mohanta, the local sarpanch who did most of the follow-up work on her behalf, in an interview with this author.

She also did all she could for rail connection between Rairangpur and Baripada, the district headquarters, and between Badampahar and Keonjhar. Unfortunately, however, neither of the two projects is complete yet.[2] 'Now that she is the President, the people of the area are hopeful that both these projects will be completed soon,' adds Mohanta.

Nandini Sarangi, an elderly woman voter in Aharbandh village narrates an anecdote from the time when Murmu was on campaign trail. 'There was no power connection in our village. When she arrived in our village to seek votes, I went up to her, holding a dibiri in the hand, and told her, "You have come to seek our votes. And we shall give you our votes, but only if you ensure power to the village." She assured me she will. And she did,' she says and then adds, rather philosophically, 'That's why she is the President of India today.'

She used the Local Area Development (LAD) funds due to her as an MLA judiciously to provide basic amenities to many villages. Being a very religious person, Murmu paid particular attention to renovation, expansion and beautification of religious places in her constituency. 'The temple that you see today was constructed entirely with funds sanctioned by her,' proclaims the priest of the Maa Banadurga temple in Badampahar, speaking to this author. 'The statue of the Goddess used to be worshipped in the open before she intervened and arranged for funds for the construction of the temple,' he adds. Since encroachments threatened the jahers, Murmu also sanctioned funds for the construction of boundary walls around many of them.

Manoranjan Murmu, the headmaster of the ME school where Murmu once studied, is all praise for the illustrious ex-student of his school. 'It was courtesy her that I got an opportunity to see the inside of the Odisha Assembly. It was through her efforts that my village Jaipur got an Ayurvedic hospital. She also got books worth about three-and-a-half lakh rupees for the Netaji Club in my village,' says Murmu, who was in college at the time.

What endeared her to the people most was her humility. 'Ego is alien to her. During the annual function of the school, we had invited her as a guest on the second day. The guest for the inaugural day was Sudam Marandi, the local MP who was with the JMM. But Didi turned up on the first day as well. We were a little embarrassed, but she put us at ease, saying, "Please carry on. Don't bother about me. I am comfortable. How can I stay away from a function in my school when I am around?"' the headmaster says.

'There is hardly a village in the constituency which did not receive some benefit or the other when she was an MLA,' says Murmu, who belongs to a village that comes under the Rairangpur constituency. 'No one has done more for the constituency than her since Independence,' adds Hari Prasad Sahu.

People in her constituency say she would honour every invitation that came her way, whether it was a birth or death in the family, a marriage or a thread ceremony or a community occasion like a Chhau (a tribal dance form) performance or a football match.

She made it a point to be by the side of people in times of grief or tragedy. 'After my wife died in a hospital in Bhubaneswar, I brought her body to Rairangpur for cremation. I was surprised to find Didi waiting for us at my home. She stayed there all day till the rituals were over without taking a morsel of food,' recalls Nigamananda Patnaik.

Murmu's bonding with the people was natural and not a PR exercise. It came from a deep empathy with the people and a genuine desire to do the best she could to provide succour to them. Her aides say she has this uncanny knack of remembering the names of even those she has met just once. What endeared her to the people most was that she did not allow ministerial protocol to come between her and her people.

With her stellar record as a minister for four years, it was only natural that she was fielded from her constituency for a second successive time in the 2004 elections. Chief Minister Naveen Patnaik had dissolved the Assembly a year ahead of its term and opted to have Assembly polls simultaneously with the parliamentary elections. The first time in 2000 was a virtual cakewalk. But this time, she had a real tough battle on her hands as she had two formidable opponents: Ramchandra Murmu of the JMM and Laxman Majhi of the Congress. She scraped through with the narrowest of margins, defeating her nearest rival Murmu by a mere forty-two votes. Murmu, however, has no regrets today about losing that particular election. 'Who knows, she might have never become the President of India had she lost that election. I am happy that I lost and unwittingly contributed to her anointment as the President. She has done all of us, irrespective of party affiliations, proud,' he told the media the day the result of the presidential elections was announced.

This was the election when Murmu met Modi, who was the CM of Gujarat and the rising star in the BJP, for the first time. The occasion was an election rally in Rairangpur where she, along with Bhagirathi Majhi, the BJP candidate from the Mayurbhanj Lok Sabha seat, shared the dais with Modi. It was the beginning of a long-term relationship that saw Modi choose Murmu as the party's presidential candidate eighteen years later.

Despite her excellent performance as minister in the previous term, however, Murmu was not made a minister the second time around. The decision had to do with the internal dynamics of the BJP. The ministerial berth this time went to her junior in college, Surama Padhy, who had won the election from the Ranpur constituency in Khurda district. (She had lost the 2000 elections by a narrow margin.) A prominent leader of the party, Surama had already served a three-year term as national president of the BJP Mahila Morcha (Women's Front) from 2000 to 2003. 'Though she lost out on a ministerial berth, there was not a trace of rancour in her. She remained the good friend she always was to me,' says Surama.

With no ministerial responsibilities to bother about, Murmu devoted herself completely to discharging her responsibilities as an MLA instead, both inside and outside the Assembly. Her first term as an MLA had given her a fair idea about the nuances and intricacies of Assembly proceedings. She used all of that and built on it to earn a reputation as a very active member of the House. She never missed Assembly proceedings. She participated in almost all debates in the House and made forceful interventions during the Zero Hour. 'Murmu Didi was the most active member of the House. What marked her out was her meticulous preparation before every debate and intervention. Pick up the proceedings on any starred question asked by her in the House from old records and it will be instantly apparent how much of preparation had gone into it. She would always carry a notebook in her vanity bag in which she would jot down notes and points,' says Surama.

Those who watched her from close quarters during those days say Murmu was not the kind who would while away time in pointless gossip and banter so common in the Assembly lobby. She would always be busy with something or the other; either sitting with a minister or an officer in the secretariat to pursue a matter related to her constituency or busy preparing for a debate in the House. Small talk was anathema to her.

Murmu's name would constantly figure in the list of speakers in discussions on the demands of various departments during the budget session. She would painstakingly collate facts and data and pose frequent questions on issues related to her constituency as well as those that affect the people of the state. The then Speaker of the Assembly, the erudite Sarat Kumar Kar, took a particular liking to Murmu and always gave her an opportunity to speak during debates in the Assembly. Her name was among the first to be ticked when the House mourned the death of a former member or an eminent personality or paid homage to great personalities during their birth or death anniversary.

Murmu's exemplary legislative performance earned her the Nilakantha Award as the best legislator in 2007. Significantly, she was the first woman recipient of the coveted award. It was a crowning glory for the shy girl of Uparbeda who had dared to dream and pursued her dreams with dogged determination.

Freed of ministerial duties, Murmu now had more time on her hands to look after the interests of her constituents. When the House was not in session, she would spend most of her time in her constituency, going from village to village, listening to the people's grievances and trying to solve them to the best of her ability.

The win in 2004, however, was going to be the last election Murmu won—till she won the election for the post of President in July 2022, that is. On the eve of the simultaneous Lok Sabha and Assembly polls in 2009, BJD supremo Naveen Patnaik unilaterally severed the eleven-year alliance with the BJP and decided to go it alone, catching the saffron party completely off guard. During seat-sharing talks with the BJP earlier, the BJD had said the 4:3 ratio that had been followed since the formation of the alliance in 1998 was no longer tenable in view of the ground realities and asked its alliance partner to settle for a lesser number of seats for both Assembly and parliamentary elections. Not prepared for this sudden change of tack by its alliance partner—and that too with barely weeks to go before the polls—the BJP central leadership sent Rajya Sabha MP Chandan Mitra as a special emissary to persuade Patnaik to stay with the status quo, but he did not relent.

The change in the BJD strategy was widely attributed to Pyari Mohan Mohapatra, Patnaik's Man Friday at the time, nicknamed 'Chanakya'. The all-powerful retired bureaucrat, who had once been the principal secretary to Biju Patnaik, apparently convinced his boss that the BJP was merely piggybacking on the BJD's support base to get a disproportionate share of seats in the Assembly and the Lok Sabha. The severance of ties would work in the BJD's favour and the party would win a comfortable majority on its own, besides a majority of the twenty-one parliamentary seats in the state, he told Naveen.

And the results of the elections vindicated the soundness of Mohapatra's assessment as the BJD went on to win a thumping majority in the Assembly elections, clinching 103 out of the 147 constituencies (more than the two alliance partners won together in 2004) with a vote share of 38.86 per cent, besides fourteen of the twenty-one Lok Sabha seats. In stunning contrast, the BJP, which had no less than thirty-two seats in the outgoing Assembly, was reduced to a mere six, the same as independents, with a vote share of just 15.05 per cent. Even more ignominious was its performance in the parliamentary elections. As against the seven seats it had won in 2004 in alliance with the BJD, the saffron party drew a blank when it fought the polls alone in 2009. It was a timely reality check for the BJP, which had fallen from cloud nine to terra firma after the alliance with the BJD fell through.

Murmu was among those in the BJP who suffered the brunt of this bitter falling out between the two estranged partners. Fielded as the BJP candidate from the Mayurbhanj Lok Sabha constituency in 2009, she was relegated to the third position, winning 1,40,770 votes (17.1 per cent), behind Laxman Tudu of the BJD who won 2,56,648 votes (31.1 per cent) and Sudam Marandi of JMM who managed 1,90,470 votes (23.1 per cent). The dissolution of the alliance with the BJD was, of course, the primary reason for her defeat in 2009. But her supporters aver that she would have won despite the fallout with the BJD had she been fielded from the Rairangpur Assembly constituency, which she had nursed very well during her two terms as MLA, instead of the Mayurbhanj Lok Sabha constituency. With seven Assembly seats and a vastly larger number of voters, the Lok Sabha election was an altogether different ball game, they point out.

The claim by her supporters, however, appears specious in view of what happened five years later in 2014, which turned out to be the last direct election Murmu fought in her political career (not counting the presidential election eight years later). She was fielded by the BJP from her old Assembly seat of Rairangpur in this election but lost to Saiba Sushil Kumar Hansdah of the BJD by a margin of 15,556 votes. Her popularity in her constituency and connect with the people could not have dwindled so much in five years as to warrant a defeat by such a large margin.

However, as later events would prove, it was the defeat in the 2014 Assembly elections that paved her way to Raisina Hills eight years later. In the run-up to this election, the BJD, in its efforts to decimate its estranged partner and return to power with an even bigger margin than it did in 2009, had begun poaching BJP leaders with winning prospect. It had already netted Golak Bihari Nayak, who had won from the

Udala constituency in Mayurbhanj in 2000 and was a ministerial colleague of Murmu from 2000 to 2004. Having lost to Srinath Soren of the BJD in 2009, Nayak readily accepted the bait offered by the BJD in the build-up to the 2014 elections and went on to win. There were several others who did the same, and were rewarded for their decision. Emissaries were also sent to Murmu to persuade her to join the BJD.

But Murmu herself was undecided. She consulted her party colleagues, including close associate Nabin Ram, on the matter. 'I advised her against joining the BJD. I told her she was free to join the ruling party, but she should not expect her supporters to switch sides with her,' says Ram. Still unable to make up her mind, she went to her mentor and senior BJP leader Rabindra Nath Mohanta and sought her advice on the matter. Mohanta advised her against leaving the BJP and joining BJD. And that clinched the issue for her. She politely declined the offer made by the BJD.

'I had talked to Murmu over the phone while she was with Rabindra Nath Mohanta at the latter's residence to consult him on whether to join the BJD. She told me Mohanta had advised her to stay put in the BJP and not join the BJD and that is what she was going to do,' senior Baripada-based senior journalist Kalyan Kumar Sinha told this author.

It is possible that in the final analysis, it was the strong personal bonding she had developed with local

BJP leaders and workers, rather than cold political calculation, that persuaded Murmu to say 'No' to the BJD offer. Right through her personal tragedies, it was her party colleagues who had stood by her, consoling her and preventing her from slipping into depression. Nabin Ram rubbishes efforts by the ruling party, initiated after she was named as the presidential candidate, to project the BJD supremo as the 'elder brother' of Murmu, saying, 'They are now circulating an old photo showing Didi tying rakhi on Naveen Patnaik's hands. But where was the "brother" when she lost, one after another, her husband and two sons? Naveen neither himself came to console her nor sent anyone on his behalf. In fact, he vigorously campaigned against his "sister" in the elections in both 2009 and 2014.' However, Murmu herself addressed Naveen as her 'rakhi brother' and thanked him for backing her even before she asked for support when she visited Bhubaneswar and met MPs and MLAs to seek support for her in the presidential election.

Had she taken the bait offered by the BJD, it was a foregone conclusion that she would have won from Rairangpur, possibly with a handsome margin, given Naveen Patnaik's growing popularity in the state and the BJD's expanding footprint in the area. In all probability, she would have also become a minister, maybe even got a Cabinet rank, given her excellent rapport with the CM. But there was no way she could have become the President of India.

It was a classic case of 'losing the battle to win the war'.

# 8

# Tragic Turn

After 2009, not only did Murmu's political career start going downhill, a series of tragedies in the family shattered her. Within a span of just four years beginning 2010, she lost five members of her family—her two sons, husband, brother and mother—to a variety of causes. A lesser mortal would have found it extremely difficult to survive these back-to-back tragedies but not Murmu. It is a testimony to her fortitude in the face of great adversity that she not only took these soul-crushing, morale-sapping personal tragedies and grief in her stride but pulled herself up to devote herself to the service of humankind.

First, she lost her eldest son, Laxman, who was barely twenty-five at the time, on 25 October 2010, under mysterious circumstances. There are several versions doing the rounds about what exactly had happened, but no one knows the truth for sure. What, however, is known is that Laxman, who was staying with her uncle and aunty in Bhubaneswar, had returned home late in the night after attending a party with his friends. But he was taken ill and was taken to the hospital in the morning where he was declared dead. Murmu, who was in Riarangpur at the time, rushed to Bhubaneswar on hearing about her elder son's illness, but it was too late by then.

Recalling that tragic incident, Delha Soren, Murmu's close friend from her college days, says, 'On hearing about Laxman's death, all of us who were close to Murmu rushed to the hospital. Murmu, who was in Rairangpur at the time, had already been informed and she was on her way to Bhubaneswar. We were all anxious to know when she would arrive, but no one was keen to call her. Finally, it fell on me to dial her. She was understandably disconsolate and shouted at me, "My son died. Yet, none of you did anything about it." As a mother myself, I understood her anguish and did not take it amiss. Once she reached the hospital, she started sobbing. We had a tough time consoling her.'

The untimely death of her eldest son in the prime of youth left Murmu numb. She lost the zest for life and went into a shell. She stopped going out completely and even skipped her meals frequently. Her friends, well-wishers and party colleagues did the best they could to get her out of the state of depression she had sunk into. They persuaded her to start going out and meeting people but to no avail.

Among the many people who met her at her Rairangpur residence during this period was Prahallad Dora, who was the Deputy Speaker of the Odisha Assembly from 2004 to 2009 when Murmu was a minister. Concerned, Dora, who was her party colleague, advised her to visit the Prajapita Brahma Kumaris Ishwariya Vishwa Vidyalaya Centre in town. A visit to the centre would help her get over her state of inner turmoil and calm her down, he reasoned. He also requested the authorities there to involve her in their activities and help her come out of her shell. The sustained persuasion worked and Murmu finally visited the centre. As subsequent events would prove, that visit changed the course of her life.

'Murmu Didi had visited our centre on a few occasions earlier too but only as a guest. But she had never gone deep into the Brahma Kumari philosophy and way of life earlier. Mr Dora came to our centre and requested us to involve her in our activities. The next morning, he sent his vehicle to the centre and we went to Murmu Didi's place to invite her. She came, listened to the morning "Murali" and sat through the meditation session. For the first few days, it was obvious that she was finding it hard to take her mind off her personal tragedy and focus on the activities completely, which was perfectly understandable given that the wound was still raw. But it was clear that she loved the ambience of the meditation centre. She told her friends and party colleagues that she felt an inner peace and tranquility at the meditation centre,' Sister Minati of the centre told this writer over the phone, recalling those days.

Soon, she enrolled for a seven-day course on spiritualism offered by the Vishwavidyalaya (university) and became a regular at the centre. She started following the Brahma Kumari way of life, getting up at 3.30 a.m. and doing her yoga and meditation, a routine she follows even now. She not only shunned non-vegetarian food but even onion and garlic in the vegetarian fare that she consumed in deference to the Brahma Kumari way of life. In due course, she created her own prayer and meditation room at home. She also started accompanying members of the centre to nearby villages and advised people to follow the Brahma Kumari way of life, telling them about her own experience of how it had helped her come out of depression.

This was the beginning of a lifelong association with the Brahma Kumaris for Murmu, who has visited Mount Abu in Rajasthan, the headquarters of the organization, and all other major centres of the denomination in the years since then. She has rarely missed the annual religious jamboree at Mount Abu, not even when she was the Governor of Jharkhand. And she has gratefully acknowledged the contribution of the organization in rescuing her from the depths of despondency and giving her a purpose in life in every interview she has given.

One of the first things she did after hearing the news about her nomination as the NDA's presidential candidate on the night of 21 June 2022 was to spend a good half an hour in the meditation room at her home and thank the 'Baba'. 'I must have been chosen to do some good work for mankind,' she told Sister Supriya and Sister Minati when they met her the next morning to congratulate her on her nomination. When she stayed overnight in Bhubaneswar en route to New Delhi to file her nomination the next day, it was not a five-star hotel but the Brahma Kumari centre in the city that her dinner and breakfast came from.

The untimely death of her elder son was only the beginning of a period of great personal loss for Murmu. A little over two years later, on 2 January 2013 to be precise, she lost her second son, Biranchi, nicknamed Sipun, in a road accident. But by then, her foray into spiritualism had steeled her sufficiently and given her an inner strength not to be overwhelmed by the loss of her second son. 'When I went to meet her the day after the death of her second son, I was amazed at how calm and tranquil she looked. While the others in the family were sobbing, there was not a drop of tear in her eyes. She just sat there, quiet and unflustered. There was talk of possible foul play in the death of her son. But she appeared to be completely oblivious of it. It seemed she had attained the state of *sthitapragyan* [a state of being beyond joy and sorrow] that our scriptures talk about,' recalls her college mate and party colleague Surama Padhy in a chat with this biographer.

Her husband Shyam Charan, however, could not take the death of their second son in his stride like her and went into depression. Soon, he fell sick with a severe bout of jaundice. As his health deteriorated, he was admitted to Kalinga Hospital in Bhubaneswar. But he never recovered and breathed his last on 1 August 2014. She bore it with the same stoicism that she had displayed at the time of her second son's death. That was not all. Soon after the death of Sipun, his wife, who was pregnant at the time, had a miscarriage. After this, her parents took her home. Murmu pleaded with them to allow her to stay back with her, but they did not relent.

Around the same time, Murmu also lost her elder brother Bhagat Charan Tudu and her mother Singo Tudu. But she was philosophical about these back-to-back tragedies. 'Life is like a water bubble. You never know when you will die. And there is no particular age to die. Not everyone dies in ripe old age. There is nothing you can do about it. But what you can do is to live—and struggle—without losing your equanimity. Joy and sorrow are both transitory. As children, we think we can't live without our parents. But we do, don't we? God has given the human mind the ability to take everything in stride,' she told her interviewer Dr Samanta later.

Murmu is a deeply religious person. As someone with an unshakable faith in the Hindu way of life, she believes in the concepts of karma and rebirth. 'I believe that karma is carried forward through the soul. I often wonder: why is it that gods and great souls like Krishna, Ram and Buddha are born into royal families? It's the result of their karma in the previous birth. One must face both joy and sorrow without allowing either of them to overwhelm you. Fate does have a role, but what really matters is one's karma.' This is how she sums up her philosophy of life.

Though she has remained faithful to the Brahma Kumari way of life, she believes in all religious and spiritual sects. She is a great devotee of Lord Jagannath, the presiding deity of Odisha, who epitomizes the concepts of classless humanity and universal brotherhood. She never misses an opportunity to visit the world-famous Lord Jagannath temple in Puri. Her personal driver Narendra told this author that she

once visited the abode of the Lord incognito in the
dead of the night just to witness the 'Bada Singhara'
Besha[1] of the deity. Everywhere she has gone and in
every speech she has made, she has hailed the essence
of the Jagannath cult. The first thing she did when she
visited her home state for the first time after becoming
President was to leave for Puri immediately after
landing at the Bhubaneswar airport and offer prayers
to the Lord.

Speaking at a conference titled Ama Utkarsha
Odisha in Mumbai organized by the Maharashtra
Odia Welfare Association on 23 February 2019 while
she was Governor of Jharkhand, Murmu had dwelt
extensively on the centrality of Lord Jagannath to the
Odia identity. She had also stressed on the tribal origins
of the Lord, which perhaps is the reason she has never
seen any contradiction in believing both Marang Buru
and Lord Jagannath simultaneously. 'Lord Jagannath
is the identity of Odisha. He symbolizes tolerance,
brotherhood and liberalism. Usually, the images of
our gods and goddesses are made of stone or earth.
But the image of Lord Jagannath is an exception as it
is made of wood. The worship of wood (trees) is an
essential part of tribal belief system. So, the Lord is as
much a god of tribals as he is of Hindus, Buddhists and
Jains. The fact that Brahmins and Shudras partake of
mahaprasad sitting side by side inside the Puri temple
proves that there is no room for caste discrimination in

the Lord's scheme of things. He spreads the message of love, peace and non-violence to the whole world,' she had said on the occasion.

Her eclectic belief in matters religious can be attributed to her immense faith in the essential philosophy of the Jagannath cult. That's why she is equally at home at a Hindu religious gathering as she is in a congregation of Muslims or Christians. She has never declined an invitation to be part of any religious or spiritual gathering, be it a yoga camp by the Art of Living sect of Sri Sri Ravishankar or the birth anniversary of Thakur Anukul Chandra, the founder of the Jay Guru cult, or a conference of pastors, for that matter. Her adherence to the worship of tribal gods at the jaher has never come in the way of her belief in the Hindu gods and goddesses. Significantly, the morning after the announcement about her nomination as the presidential candidate of NDA was made, she went to the local Shiva temple and the Brahma Kumari centre before rounding off her thanksgiving tour with a visit to the jaher.

Nor has her affiliation with the BJP prevented her from enjoying the love and affection of Muslims. Sitting at the Badampahar railway station, Sheikh Mehmood, one of her trusted foot soldiers in the area, points to the masjid across the road before saying, 'She has taken lunch there many times during her visits here. She is a true Ajatashatru [someone who doesn't have an enemy], if ever there was one.' At the Raj Bhavan in Ranchi, there were cooks from all three major faiths of India and all of them were treated the same way by her. 'Madam had made it amply clear that everyone could cook for her. If there was Pradeep in the kitchen, there were also Jasim Ansari and John and all of them took turns cooking for her,' says S.S. Parihar, the man who manages the Governor's day-to-day requirements at the Raj Bhavan. She is a great believer in the 'one God, many ways' dictum.[2]

It was her unflinching, unquestioning faith in the divine design that enabled her to leave her personal tragedies, which she has described as nothing short of a 'tsunami' in her life, behind and re-dedicate herself to the cause of serving mankind. Suddenly, 'Miles to go before I sleep', the line from Robert Frost's poem 'Stopping by Woods on a Snowy Evening', which she was so fond of as a child, acquired a new meaning for her. That she could pull herself up from the depths of despair to rise to the highest office in the country is a fascinating study of what human grit and determination can achieve. Her life story is an inspiration for all those who lose their desire to live after facing similar, or even lesser, tragedies in their lives.

Murmu had lost her first child, a daughter, when the latter was just three. And now, she was left with just her second daughter, Itishree. She wanted her to get married and settle down, but Itishree was reluctant.

'What did you get after marrying, except misery?' she asked her mother. But Murmu managed to persuade her to relent. She is now happily married to Ganesh Chandra Hembram, a rugby coach. Itishree, a banker, is now a mother of two children. She now stays with her mother at Rashtrapati Bhavan after getting a transfer to New Delhi.

After the death of her two sons and husband, Murmu got her younger brother Taranisen and his wife to stay with her at her Rairangpur residence. They too now stay with her at the Rashtrapati Bhavan.

Murmu gradually returned to her social and political activities and started visiting villages in her area and meeting people again. 'Those destined to die have died. Why should those living suffer because of that? What sin have they committed?' she asked herself as she immersed herself fully in serving the people.

She fought the 2014 Assembly election as the BJP candidate from her old constituency of Rairangpur and lost to the BJD candidate, Saiba Sushil Kumar Hansdah. But like the series of personal tragedies in her life, she had, by then, acquired the equanimity to take electoral defeats too in her stride.

# 9

# People's Governor

After losing the 2014 Assembly election, Murmu spent most of her time looking after the affairs of the BJP in Mayurbhanj in her capacity as its district unit president. She had already served a three-year stint as president of the Mayurbhanj (west) BJP unit from 2010 to 2013 and was now in her second term. As a member of the National Executive Committee of the BJP's ST Morcha since 2013, she was also engaged in raising various issues related to tribals in the party forum.

Life was limping back to a semblance of normalcy after the series of devastating tragedies on the personal front when Murmu received a call from an officer in the Union Home ministry asking for her biodata. The official did not reveal the purpose, but Murmu guessed it might have something to do with her possible appointment as chairperson of some corporation. There was speculation that her name was being considered as a member of the National Commission for Scheduled Tribes (NCST). Soon thereafter, there was an Intelligence Bureau (IB) inquiry into her police record to check if she had any cases pending against her, but Murmu was yet not aware of what the whole exercise was about.

After the inquiry was completed, she got a call from an IB official informing her that there was some 'good news' coming her way. Shortly thereafter, she got to know what the 'good news' was. It turned out to be something she had not imagined even in her wildest dreams—she was being appointed the Governor of Jharkhand. There couldn't have been better news for someone who had lost two consecutive elections.

The nature of gubernatorial postings in India is such that most people are appointed Governor in states far away from their home states. They thus need some time to acclimatize themselves to their new environment—the language, the culture and the political ground realities of the state. But that was not the case with Murmu; she was completely at home at the Raj Bhavan in Ranchi from day one since she was already familiar with the state and its people. For one thing, she had spent considerable time with her husband, who had served as a bank officer at various places in Jharkhand. She also had several relatives living or working at various places in Jharkhand, including Ranchi, the state capital. Murmu's home town of Rairangpur is much closer to Ranchi (195 kilometres), just a four-hour drive, than it is to Bhubaneswar, the capital city of Odisha, a distance of 288 kilometres (a six-hour drive). As a prominent Santhal leader from Mayurbhanj, she already knew the 'first family' of the JMM since all three children of party patriarch Shibu Soren, including incumbent CM Hemant Soren, are married to Santhal families based in her home district.

For another, she came from more or less the socio-political-cultural milieu that she was walking into as Governor. Like Odisha, Jharkhand is a state with a substantial tribal population (Odisha: 22.85 per cent,[1] Jharkhand: 26.21 per cent[2]).

Like Odisha again, the Santhals are the dominant tribe in Jharkhand. Mayurbhanj, her home district, borders Jharkhand and is one of three northern districts in Odisha—the other two being Keonjhar and Sundargarh—that were sought to be included in the proposed new state by the proponents of a separate state of Jharkhand. The JMM pursued the demand for the inclusion of these three districts even after the formation of the Jharkhand state in 2000 and continued to enjoy considerable electoral support in the area, especially in Mayurbhanj, with Sudam Marandi winning the Mayurbhanj Lok Sabha seat on JMM ticket in the 1999 parliamentary elections. It is another matter that the Jharkhand movement in Mayurbhanj fizzled out after Marandi, who was the president of the Odisha state unit of JMM, defected to the ruling BJD along with five other prominent leaders of the party on the eve of the 2014 elections. Murmu thus settled into her job without any of the problems of unfamiliarity that most Governors face at their places of posting.

In nominating Murmu as Governor, the BJP top brass was essentially trying to assuage the hurt feelings of the tribals, who had not taken kindly to its decision to make Raghubar Das, a non-tribal, the CM of the state after the Assembly elections in December 2014. The choice of Das, the first non-tribal CM of Jharkhand, was, in a way, forced on the BJP since the other major contender for the post, former CM Arjun Munda, had lost the election from Kharsawan. And Babulal Marandi, the first CM of Jharkhand after the state was carved out of Bihar in 2000, had already left the BJP after falling out with the party leadership and had formed his own party, Jharkhand Vikas Morcha (Prajatantrik). (He is now back in the BJP fold and is the leader of the Opposition in the Jharkhand Assembly.) As a five-time MLA from Jamshedpur (east) constituency, Das thus emerged as the strongest candidate for the top post among the thirty-seven elected on a BJP ticket.

However, the tribals of Jharkhand, who constitute the biggest chunk of the electorate at 26.21 per cent in the state,[3] could not care less for the internal dynamics of the BJP. They were just angry that a non-tribal was heading the government in a state that had been carved out of Bihar essentially as a homeland for them. As resentment among the tribals grew, the BJP leadership hit upon the idea of making a tribal the Governor of the state in deference to the sentiments of the tribals. And Murmu had just the right credentials for the job. After all, she was a tribal—and a Santhal at that. Her appointment as Governor, therefore, was expected to douse the flames of anger among the tribals in general and the Santhals, the most populous tribe in the state, in particular. The fact that she was going to be the first woman to become the Governor of Jharkhand also must have weighed with the BJP think tank as it provided the party strategists an opportunity to sell it as an exercise in women's empowerment.

Murmu was not just the first woman to become the Governor of Jharkhand, she was also the first Governor of the state to complete the full term of five years. In fact, her tenure lasted a little over six years— from 18 May 2015 to 12 July 2021—because of the extraordinary circumstances created by the Covid-19 pandemic. During those six years, she endeared herself to the tribals and won their lasting gratitude with her unflinching commitment to their welfare and an unwavering desire to stand up for their rights. 'She did more for the tribals of the state during her stint as Governor than any CM had done before,' Ranchi-based senior journalist Ravi Prakash told this writer in a personal interview.

Murmu's nomination as Governor of Jharkhand may have been an exercise in firefighting for the BJP high command at the time. But by the time she laid down office six years later, she had etched her name in the minds of people as the finest Governor the state has had in the twenty-two years of its existence. It is hard to find anyone in the state—whether a commoner or a big shot, someone from the ruling party or the Opposition—who talks in anything but the most glowing terms about her. At a time when most Governors are facing charges of partisanship, she was a Governor who enjoyed the love and respect of the people on both sides of the political divide. She earned that respect with her even-handedness in dealing with politicians belonging to the ruling and opposition parties. In many ways, it was her stellar performance as the Governor of Jharkhand that later paved her way to the Rashtrapati Bhavan.

For the first four-and-a-half years of her tenure, the BJP-AJSU (All Jharkhand Students Union) coalition government headed by Raghubar Das was in the saddle. For the next year and a half of her stint, she had to work with the JMM-Congress-RJD alliance government headed by Hemant Soren, which came to power in the November/December 2019 elections. Curiously though, she enjoyed the best of relations with the Soren government while she had a serious run-in with the government led by the BJP, the party she belonged to before becoming Governor, on the issue of tribal land rights.

What brought matters to a head was an amendment proposed by the Raghubar Das government to two laws enacted to protect the land rights of the tribals: the British-era Chotanagpur Tenancy Act (CNTA), 1908 and the Santhal Parganas Tenancy (supplementary provisions) Act (SPTA), 1949. With the objective of preventing tribal land alienation, both these Acts barred the sale or transfer of tribal land to non-tribals. Even while allowing sale of land by a tribal to a fellow tribal, it barred the use of such land for non-agricultural purposes.

There was stiff opposition to the two amendment Bills when they were moved in the Assembly on 23 November 2016, with the Opposition alleging that the proposed amendments would only hasten the process of tribal land alienation. The two Bills were passed by the Assembly through voice vote without any discussion in three minutes flat amid an Opposition boycott. Spontaneous protests against the amendments broke out on the streets of Ranchi and several other places in the state the same day and gathered momentum over the following days. Scores of memorandums calling for withholding of accent to the proposed amendment Bills were submitted to Governor Murmu.

At the height of the tussle over the two amendment Bills, Governor Murmu took an indirect dig at the CM without naming him, says Supriyo Bhattacharya, JMM general secretary. 'Speaking on the occasion of the Foundation Day of the Jharkhand Assembly, the Governor said, "Governments cannot act out of arrogance. They have to respect public sentiments and take into consideration the views of the Opposition." Though she did not name anyone, there was no doubt in the minds of those present as to who she was referring to. Earlier, she had said much the same thing in the Assembly too,' he says.

The primary bone of contention was the proposed insertion of Section 21(B) in the CNT Act—and Section 13(A) in the SPT Act—empowering the state government to frame rules to 'regulate the non-agricultural use of land in such geographical area and for such uses as notified by the state government'. Critics of the amendment were of the view that this was akin to handing over tribal land to non-tribals for commercial exploitation.

In its defence, the government pointed to the proviso 'but the Right of Ownership (Malikana Hak), title and interest on the land when its use changes from agricultural to non-agricultural purposes shall continue to remain with the Raiyat as per the relevant provisions of CNT Act, 1908 as before the enactment of this amendment'.[4] Those opposed to the amendment said this was a misnomer since there was no definition of 'Right of Ownership' in the original Act. They pointed out that the beneficial restrictions of Sections 47, 48, 71(A), 240, 241 and 242 of the CNT Act, 1908 which provide protection of the land rights of tribals, apply only to 'occupancy raiyats' of the tribal community— those who hold land for cultivation. In the absence of a redefinition of a 'raiyat' and corresponding amendments to the sections mentioned above, the protection offered by them will not be available to the tribal raiyat the moment the land is used for non-agricultural purposes, they said. Similarly, the protection offered by Sections 20(1) and 20(5) of the SPT Act will no longer be available to a 'tribal raiyat' once the land is used for non-agricultural purposes.

Among the scores of memorandums and representations calling for withholding accent to the Bills submitted to the Governor was a letter written by Dr Rameshwar Oraon, chairperson of the NCST. Apart from pointing out the inconsistencies and incongruities of the proposed amendment, it also said that the Bills violated the provisions of the Panchayat (Extension to Scheduled Areas) Act (PESA), 1996, since they do away with the mandatory approval of the Gram Sabha before making changes in the land use pattern.

The apprehensions in the minds of those opposed to the amendments had a historical basis. It is, therefore, necessary to go a bit into the history of the landmass presently known as the state of Jharkhand. This region used to be an almost exclusive preserve of tribals till around the second half of the eighteenth century, when land-hungry peasants and rapacious traders from nearby areas began settling there. Using all possible means, such as coercion, trickery litigation and liquor, these new settlers started usurping the land belonging to tribals, reducing them from landowners to tenants. Following a series of tribal uprisings against this wanton exploitation by outsiders—the prominent among them being the revolt by Tilka Manjhi in 1789, the Kol uprising of 1831–32, the Santhal revolt (also known as the Hul revolt) of 1855–57 and the Birsa Ulgulan of 1895–1900—the Britishers enacted a host of laws with the primary objective of preventing tribal land alienation. Among them were the Chota Nagpur Tenures Act, 1869; the Santhal Parganas Settlement Regulation, 1872; the Santhal Parganas Settlement Regulations, 1904, the Chota Nagpur Tenancy Act, 1908; and the Santhal Parganas Settlement Record Revision Regulations, 1939. After Independence, the Government of India enacted the Santhal Parganas Tenancy Act, 1949, with the same objective.

Despite all these legal instruments, however, the dangers of usurpation of tribal land through trickery remains real even in present times due to the lack of education and awareness among the tribals. Hence, it was only natural that those working for protection of the land rights of tribals saw red in the amendments moved by the government. But it was a fact that there was a section even among the tribals, even if minuscule, which wanted the amendments to go through. With the spread of education and awareness, many tribals wanted to shift from cultivation to other avenues of income. But the two laws in question came in the way for any tribal keen to use their land for setting up a shop or starting a small business since they barred non-agricultural use of the land. Banks refused to sanction loans on the same grounds. For the backers of the amendment, therefore, there was a case for removing the impediments posed by the two Acts enacted several decades ago.

J.B. Tubid, who was the Home secretary of the state at the time, says the intentions of the government were honest. 'Many new-age tribal youths want to start their own business. But the problem for them is that they cannot avail bank loans for their proposed venture since the law prevents mortgaging their land for non-agricultural purposes,' he told this author.

The government chose Tubid, perhaps because he was a tribal himself, to sell the amendments to the tribals. He was asked to prepare an exhaustive PowerPoint presentation (PPT) explaining why the amendments were necessary and addressing tribal gatherings at various places to win them over. Accordingly, he prepared a PPT with some forty-odd slides and went to Chaibasa, a district headquarters town, to start his campaign. But the meeting at the Pillai Hall in Chaibasa turned out to be chaotic and ended in a fiasco.

Meanwhile, Governor Murmu was in the process of assessing the desirability of giving accent to the amendment Bills by meeting various tribal leaders and talking to legal experts. As a tribal herself, she understood the dangers of tribal land passing on to non-tribal hands and was inclined towards withholding accent to the Bills. Sensing her reservations, the Raghubar Das government initiated all efforts to convince her. First, Chief Secretary Rajbala Verma, Tubid's wife, was sent as an emissary. Then it sent Tubid to make a detailed presentation on the government's point of view. The senior bureaucrat said there were enough checks and balances in the amended Acts to prevent alienation of tribal land, but Murmu was apparently not convinced. Chief Minister Das himself tried to broach the subject during a courtesy call to wish the Governor on her birthday but failed.

All these efforts, however, came to naught and the Governor returned the two Bills to the state government seeking a series of clarifications on their various provisions. 'She called the "mundas" and "mankis" [village heads] and met tribal MPs and MLAs to seek their views on the proposed amendments. There was a total of 150 objections raised against the Bills. She listened to all of them intently and was then immersed in deep contemplation for three days. I had never seen her more tense. In the end, she asked me to return the Bills to the government,' Santosh Satapathy, the Governor's principal secretary at the time, told this author. Realizing which way the wind was blowing, the government did not press the matter any further.

With that one act, Murmu won the lasting gratitude of the tribals of Jharkhand. Even Tubid, the officer who had tried to convince her about the desirability of the Bills at the time, now says it was an act of 'statesmanship'. 'It is not that the Bills had no merit. For all you know, a similar Bill may be necessary ten or twenty years from now. But the time was perhaps not ripe for the Bills at the time when they were moved. It is to her eternal credit that she saw it much before we did,' says the man, who is now a BJP leader, after taking voluntary retirement from government service.

Interestingly, an 'Advisory Committee on the Rights of Citizens, Minorities, Tribals and Excluded Areas' appointed by the Constituent Assembly under the chairmanship of Home Minister Sardar Vallabhbhai Patel had foreseen precisely such a scenario during the framing of the Constitution of India. A.V. Thakkar, the chairman of one of the sub-committees set up under the committee to look into the excluded areas in provinces other than Assam, had made the following observations: 'The importance of these special tenancy laws cannot be overstated. The history of the Santhal Parganas and Chota Nagpur was one of continuous exploitation and dispossession of the aboriginals punctuated by disorder and even rebellion until special and adequate protection was given. The special tenancy laws of Chota Nagpur and Santhal Parganas are the bulwark of the backward people. The legislatures of the future would have the power to amend, modify and even repeal those laws and the only safeguard against legislative action detrimental to the interests of the backward people is the power of the Governor to refuse accent.'[5]

One doesn't really know whether Murmu had read this far-sighted observation made by Thakkar over seven decades ago, but she did play a historic role in safeguarding the interests of the tribals of Jharkhand.

If Murmu forced the Das government to backtrack on this issue, she also bailed the same government out of a tricky situation with her act of statesmanship during the Pathalgadi movement. The movement, launched by the tribals of Khunti district in 2016, was a spontaneous reaction to two amendments to decades-old Acts—the CNT Act, 1908, and the SPT Act, 1949—passed by the Jharkhand government in November 2016 that would allow transfer of tribal land to the government for specified purposes. The tribals saw it as a move by the government to usurp their land and hand it over to private parties for commercial purposes. The amendments sought to be introduced by the Das government to the CNT Act, 1908, and the SPT Act, 1949, in November 2016 provided fuel to the raging fire and the movement born in Khunti, the birthplace of the tribal icon Birsa Munda, soon started spreading far beyond the limits of the district. In no time, it rolled out to over 200 villages spread across the four districts of Khunti, Gumla, Simdega and West Singhbhum.

The Pathalgadi movement was essentially an assertion of tribal supremacy and the disavowal of the authority of the State as well as the Constitution of India. Taking a leaf out of the PESA Act but adding its own interpretation of its provisions, it made the Gram Sabha the supreme authority in deciding all matters related to the village—jal, jangal and zameen (water, forests and land), in particular—and refused to accept the authority of the state or the central government. The leaders of the movement called upon the tribals to return their Voter ID and Aadhaar cards to the government saying they were useless in the 'republic of tribals'. They even threatened to take over schools run by various boards such as the Central Board of Secondary Education, the Council of Higher Secondary Education and state boards and run these schools under their own board where the students would be taught the glorious history and culture of tribals. 'We are the Bharat Sarkar (the Indian government). We do not recognize the central government or the state governments or the President, Prime Minister or Governor,' the tribal leaders proclaimed defiantly.[6] Large stone plaques banning the entry of outsiders, including government officials and police personnel, into the village were put up at the entry point of villages by the leaders of the movement. Even local MPs and MLAs found it difficult to enter villages that had announced what, in essence, amounted to virtual 'secession' from the Union of India. Those who defied the 'orders' were taken hostage. In short, there was complete lawlessness in the areas where the movement had taken root.

While the two ordinances promulgated by the Union government and the two amendments moved by the state government were the immediate trigger, the Pathalgadi movement was an expression of pent-up anger and exasperation against the exploitation and marginalization of tribals for decades. Given the belligerent mood of the tribals, the issue required sensitive and patient handling by the government. But instead, the Raghubar Das government adopted a confrontationist approach to the movement. Large hoardings were put up across the state terming it 'unconstitutional', 'anti-national' and worse and threatening to crush it with the full might of the State. Chief Minister Raghubar Das himself took the lead, daring the proponents of the movement to stop him from entering villages. Terming the leading lights of the movement as 'Maoists', police cracked down hard on them. Hundreds of leaders of the movement and thousands of ordinary people were arrested. Many of them were booked under the stringent sedition law.

The inevitable happened. The attitude of the tribals, belligerent to start with, hardened further after the police crackdown. Armed with traditional weapons like arrows and bows and axes, tribal youths stood guard at the entry points of villages to stop *diku*s (outsiders) from entering. At several places, government officials and policemen who sought to enter villages on official work were taken hostage by the protesters. Matters came to head when tribals took security personnel assigned to BJP MP Karia Munda. The police cracked down hard on the tribals, killing one person in firing. Cases were filed against 200 of them, including tribal rights activist Father Stan Swamy (who died in jail during the Covid pandemic for want of proper medical attention).

Let alone government officials, even policemen in the areas worst affected by the movement were a scared lot and police stations in such areas shut down by evening fearing violence. It was complete anarchy as the writ of the State simply did not run in a vast swathe of land. Having adopted a needlessly confrontationist approach on the issue from the beginning, the state government was at its wit's end as to how to arrest the growing lawlessness.

It is at this stage that Governor Droupadi Murmu decided to take matters into her hands. She called a meeting of over 700 mundas and mankis at the Raj Bhavan in which secretaries of all major departments dealing with public welfare were asked to be present. Addressing the village heads, Murmu explained to them that the Constitution provided enough safeguards for their interests to be fully protected and urged them to shun violence. Since she was a tribal herself, her words carried greater credibility for the assembled crowd than those of the government officials. She encouraged the village headmen to air all their grievances and asked the officials present to address them at the earliest.

In asking for the grievances of tribals to be addressed, she was not merely paying lip service. She followed up with officials on the work done to address the issues raised by the mundas and mankis. Her refusal to accord approval to the two amendment Bills had already endeared her to the tribals, who believed she was one of their own. Now, her sincerity in addressing their issues won their gratitude. The withdrawal of the two ordinances promulgated by the Union government and the Jharkhand government's pragmatic and sensible decision not to press ahead with the proposed amendments to the CNT and SPT Acts helped cool down tempers and the Pathalgadi movement, which had proved to be a serious headache for the Das government for nearly two years, started fizzling out in 2018. For the second time during her stint as Governor, Murmu helped prevent a situation from spiraling out of control with her tact and wisdom.

Murmu's exemplary conduct during these two episodes proved beyond doubt that she was not the 'rubber stamp' that Governors are often accused of being. She showed that she had a mind of her own and she listened to her conscience. 'At the height of the tug-of-war with the state government, she had even contemplated resigning, if matters came to a head,' says Santosh Satapathy, her principal secretary at the time. In sending back the two amendment Bills to the government, she also showed that she had the ability to rise above party loyalty as a Governor is expected to do. By helping the Das government tide over the storm called 'Pathalgadi', she displayed her statesman-like qualities.

'When she was nominated as the presidential candidate of the NDA, many people here were sceptical. "What will she do as the President?" they asked. I told them, "As Governor, she has already shown what she can do, hasn't she?" I am not a great fan of the BJP. But I fully support its decision to make her the President,' says senior journalist Ravi Prakash. 'Those who called her a "rubber stamp" in the run-up to the presidential election were grossly unfair to her,' adds former Jharkhand Home Secretary Tubid.

There was, however, much more to Murmu's six-year term as Governor than these two episodes. Her proactive role as Governor helped solve some long-pending issues in areas like education and health. Governors generally confine themselves to Raj Bhavans, going out only occasionally to grace some function or ceremony, but Murmu was an exception. She toured the state extensively, going into the remotest areas and seeing things for herself, especially in the two areas mentioned above. She paid particular attention to girls' education, which she believed was the best recipe for women's emancipation. Of the 304 Kasturba Gandhi Balika Awashiya Vidyalayas, she visited over 200 during her six-year stint as Governor. Many of these visits were unannounced so that she could see things as they are and not as dressed up for her. Security of girls was a major concern for Murmu, who ensured the required funds were sanctioned for the construction of boundary walls around all-girls' hostels. She also visited almost all public health centres (PHCs) and community health centres (CHCs) in the state to take stock of the facilities and services and moved the officials of the health department to sort out pending issues, infrastructural or otherwise. These visits helped improve the state of affairs in these institutions at the grassroots level.

Long before it became the capital of Jharkhand state, Ranchi was known for its mental hospital. Set up way back in 1918, the Central Institute of Psychiatry (CIP) is known as a premier hospital for mental health and neurosciences in the country. But the quality of mental health services on offer had gone steadily downhill over the years due to official sloth and apathy. As Governor, Murmu set her mind and soul to earning for CIP its rightful place in the country. She visited the hospital and had wide-ranging discussions with the doctors in charge to identify the issues plaguing the institute. She then sent her principal secretary Santosh Satapathy to study the state of affairs at the National Institute of Mental Health and Neuroscience (NIMHANS), Bengaluru. Satapathy reported long queues at the hospital set up in 1954, almost four decades after CIP. She felt with the right kind of infrastructure and human resources, CIP could be developed to ease the pressure on NIMHANS.

Determined to earn for CIP the status of a Centre of Excellence and an Institute of National Importance, she talked to the Union Health Secretary and even met PM Modi in this regard. She also raised the matter at the Governors' Conference convened by President Ram Nath Kovind. For better running of the hospital, she proposed CIP's merger with Ranchi University. She had already done the groundwork for full institutional autonomy to CIP by the time her term as Governor came to an end.

Her role as Chancellor of Universities is talked about in glowing terms by all those who were part of the higher education system of the state at the time. She made it a practice to hold monthly meetings of vice chancellors where the secretaries of the Higher Education, Welfare, PWD and various other departments, besides the chief secretary, the director general of police (DGP) and the development commissioner, were present. This was her way of sorting out pending issues of universities on the spot. If some university needed buildings or classrooms to be constructed, the PWD secretary was instructed to sanction the required funds for the same. If there were any security-related issues, the DGP was asked to do what was required. If there was a delay in payment of scholarships and stipends to students, the welfare secretary was asked to look into it. With meetings taking place every month, the officers were constantly on their toes to deliver the goods. She played a very proactive role in filling up of vacancies both in teaching and non-teaching posts. To tide over the shortage of teaching staff, she started recruitment of contractual teachers and enhanced their pay packets to keep them motivated. There is a provision for compensatory appointment to spouses or children of staff who die in office. But there was a backlog of eight to ten years in such appointments when she took over as Governor. In one go, she cleared forty-two such appointments. She ensured timely promotion and payment of salaries of university staff by taking up these issues with the officials of the Higher Education department on a regular basis. She asked vice chancellors of all universities to convene special meetings of the syndicate[7] on the single-point agenda of teachers' promotion. She also decreed that the service of teachers be counted from the date they joined, earning the gratitude of the teachers' community. To tide over the shortage of teaching staff, she started a system of appointing toppers as ad hoc teachers on a consolidated salary of Rs 32,000 per month since regular appointments through the Jharkhand Public Service Commission (JPSC) took ages. She also took the initiative to fill up vacancies in the JPSC. In her capacity as Chancellor of Universities and the appellate authority in matters related to universities, she played a very proactive role in solving any outstanding cases and issues and never allowed matters to linger. She prioritized solving cases, if any, against vice chancellors.

As chancellor, she paid particular attention to the Department of Tribal and Regional Languages (TRL) at Ranchi University. Though the department was set up way back in 1980, it was meandering along for years due to an acute shortage of teaching staff and lack of infrastructural facilities. The department got a complete makeover during the six years she was Governor. Long seen as a poor cousin of other departments, TRL is now the object of envy for others. It boasts a brand-new building with modern amenities constructed at a cost of Rs 3.35 crore. Simultaneously, the old building was also given a complete makeover at an expense of Rs 2.3 crore.

Talking to this author, Dr Hari Oraon, the head of the TRL department, narrates an incident that provided the trigger for the reconstruction and renovation of the old building. 'One day, she had come on a visit to TRL and was walking, along with the Higher Education secretary and other senior officials of the department, when she stumbled on a ditch created by peeling plaster on the floor. "Why is the building in such a poor state? Is it because they teach tribal languages?" she asked the Higher Education secretary. That simple question did the trick. The old building was renovated and a new one constructed, entirely due to the initiative taken by Madam Governor,' he says.

Murmu was quick to realize that the major problem plaguing TRL was an acute shortage of teaching staff. Though the department offered postgraduate and PhD programmes in as many as nine languages—four of them regional and the other five tribal—there were only sixteen sanctioned posts of teachers. She decided that each language unit of the department should have at least five teachers: a professor, two associate professors and two assistant professors. At her initiative, twenty-nine more posts were sanctioned by the government. She also ensured that the long-delayed promotion of teachers to associate professor and assistant professor rank was cleared by the government. 'As President of the teachers' association, I met her with our demands. She gave us a patient hearing and promised to take up the matter with the Higher Education department. And she did. It was entirely due to her intervention that we got what we deserved,' a grateful Prof. Khaliq Ahmed, a teacher of TRL at a college in Ranchi, told this author. When she learnt that those passing out from TRL were finding it difficult to get jobs as teachers in other universities because their degrees only mentioned MA in TRL without specifying the subjects, she ensured that the degrees issued by Ranchi University mentioned the particular subject they had done their master's in.

Prof. Oraon narrates an incident that sheds light as much on the respect with which she treated people as on the importance of TRL in her scheme of things. 'I was in New Delhi on some official work when I got a call from Prof. Anand Bhushan, former vice chancellor who was the education advisor to the Governor, asking me to attend a meeting at the Raj Bhavan the next morning where a decision was to be taken on the appointment of contractual teachers in TRL. My flight to Ranchi was in the evening. But I couldn't reach the airport in time due to a heavy traffic jam and thus missed the flight. I booked a ticket for a flight the next morning to reach Ranchi in time for the meeting. I got up at 4 a.m. and was getting ready when I received a message from the airline saying the flight was delayed due to some reason. I informed Mr Bhushan about the delay and requested him to go ahead with the meeting without me since there was no way I could reach Ranchi in time. But he said, "The Governor has said your presence is essential at the meeting. So, please rush to the Raj Bhavan straight from the airport. We shall wait for you." My flight touched down at the Birsa Munda airport at 11 a.m., the time the meeting was scheduled, and I asked the driver to drive as fast as he could. When I reached the Raj Bhavan, I was surprised to find that there was none of the usual security paraphernalia. The guard at the gate just asked me if I was Hari Oraon and when I nodded, he allowed me to go in. The officials at the reception were eagerly waiting for me and immediately escorted me to the conference hall. They taunted me saying, "It seems you are above the Governor." When I got in, the Governor welcomed me with a smile and the meeting commenced,' says Prof. Oraon. 'I doubt if TRL would get the same importance in future,' he adds.

If Murmu is fondly remembered as the 'People's Governor' in Ranchi, there is a good reason for it. By common consensus, she was the most accessible

Governor the young state has seen. Just about anyone could seek—and get—an audience with her. The imposing walls of the Raj Bhavan failed to prevent her from reaching out to people. Not just politicians, commoners, too, could get an appointment with her. Those who met her or watched her from close quarters during her six-year tenure doubt if there was a more accessible Governor anywhere in the country. 'It was easier to get an audience with her than it was to meet the local BDO,' Brijbhushan Bhagat, a Ranchi resident, joked. While what Bhagat said was more in jest than anything else, everyone this author spoke to in Ranchi and elsewhere vouched for the fact that it was not very far from the truth.

Official protocol, however, often came in the way of her desire to be among people. Her long-time personal driver Narendra Lohar recalls an incident where she gave the slip to her security personnel to go to the Prajapita Brahma Kumaris Ishwariya Vishwa Vidyalaya centre during a visit to her home town Rairangpur when she was Governor. 'Madam called me over the phone to say she wanted to visit the Brahma Kumari centre and asked me to be ready on the wheel. She obviously did not want the sanctity of the place violated by sirens blaring and armed policemen following her. I don't know how she managed to dodge the prying eyes of her security personnel, but she got on to the vehicle and we drove off before anyone could realize what was happening. The security people were at their wit's end as we went off the radar for about half an hour. When we returned, she asked me to drop her at her residence and drive off immediately without stopping,' Lohar says with a chuckle.

For people from Murmu's home state Odisha in general and her home town Rairangpur in particular, the doors of Raj Bhavan were always open. It is hard to find anyone in Rairangpur—even mere acquaintances—who didn't visit her at the Raj Bhavan. A large number of people from her area were present as guests when she was sworn in as the Governor of Jharkhand on 18 May 2016. And there was a steady stream of visitors from her home state right through her six-year term. Gayatri Sahu, a homemaker in Hatbadla, just can't stop talking about her humility and generosity when she was Governor. 'We stayed in the Raj Bhavan for five days. She would personally enquire about our comfort and well-being each day. "What will you have for lunch?" she would ask us and then instruct her kitchen staff accordingly. She showed me around the Raj Bhavan. "This is where Prime Minister Narendra Modi stayed during his visit to Ranchi, this where Amit Shah stayed," she would tell me as she took me around the many rooms in the Raj Bhavan. We have never been to a royal palace, but we certainly felt like royalty for those five days. The children just cannot stop talking about it,' she gushes.

Jitendra Nath Pattanayak, a Bhubaneswar-based senior journalist, recounts an experience that goes to show how one could get an appointment with the 'People's Governor' even at short notice. 'Along with two other journalist friends, I had gone to attend the International Tourism Festival in Ranchi at the invitation of the Jharkhand government. We were lodged at a luxury hotel in the city. Since we were in Ranchi, we thought a meeting with the Governor would just be the icing on the cake but were not too sure if we would get an appointment with her at such short notice. We called her PA, Mr Mohanta, who initially said "No". But when we told him that we were from Odisha and insisted, he said he would check with the Governor and get back. And get back he did, within a few minutes, to inform us that she had agreed to meet us. We rushed to the Raj Bhavan immediately and were pleasantly surprised to find that Madam Murmu was waiting for us. She was most cordial and served us cashews and other snacks. Though we had been granted just 15 minutes, we ended up talking for an hour and half discussing a variety of issues. I presented her my book on the lifestyle and culture of Gond tribals titled *Dangar Uhade Jahna*. She flipped through the book and then told me, "Why don't you write a book on the Santhals of Mayurbhanj? I will extend all possible help." I am happy to tell you I have started working on the book proposed by her,' says Pattanayak.

Ramachandra Murmu, a friend of her husband, met her thrice while she was Governor. 'Every time I was in Ranchi in connection with some work, I would give her a call and she would ask me to come over. I used to hesitate, thinking she must be busy. But she made light of it and insisted that I come and have a cup of tea with her, if nothing else,' he says.

Murmu invited almost all her friends and relatives to come over and spend some time with her at the Raj Bhavan. Among the many people who stayed with her during her six years as Governor was a group of five friends from her school and college days. Recalling the wonderful time the group had during those five days, Gayamani Besra, her senior in college and lifelong friend, says, 'We were pleasantly surprised to find that she had not changed one bit after becoming Governor and still remained the simple, fun-loving girl we knew in childhood. The five days we spent at the Raj Bhavan in March 2021 were real fun. She would sing and dance and play Antakshari with us. While she had become a strict vegetarian, she made sure we had our share of non-veg food during our stay. One day, one of us suggested that we have food on Saal leaf plates, just as we used to do in our childhood, for a change instead of the elegant steel or china clay utensils on which food is served at the Raj Bhavan. Droupadi lapped up the idea wholeheartedly and took the lead in stitching plates out of Saal leaves procured from the Raj Bhavan premises. I was surprised to find that the plates made by her were the most rounded and flawless!'

While she did host many people from her home state, her primary commitment was to the people of Jharkhand. And she met people from all walks of life. 'A Governor is rarely seen. But she was an exception. She went out of her way to see people and in turn be seen by them,' says former top bureaucrat Tubid. 'She would listen to the problems and grievances with rapt attention and do the best she could to sort their issues out. Sometimes, people didn't even need to see her to get their problems solved. She would hear about or read about someone in distress in the newspapers and then seek him or her out to provide succour.'

Stories of her compassion and benevolence are legends. There was this poor, differently abled tribal woman named Luguni Munda, who had been kidnapped and kept in captivity by Maoists before being impregnated and abandoned by them. She gave birth to a baby and was in dire straits when Murmu read about her in the newspapers. Murmu invited the woman to the Raj Bhavan, who walked in on crutches carrying her baby in her lap. After patiently listening to her tragic story, she went out of her way to help the woman in every possible way. At her initiative, Luguni was given a ration card, a house under the Pradhan Mantri Awas Yojana (PMAY) and a tube well to boot. She made arrangements for her son, when he grew up, to be admitted to the missionary-run Loyola School in Chaira, near Dalbhumgarh, and sanctioned money from the Governor's discretionary funds for payment of his tuition and hostel fees up to Class X. On special occasions like Diwali, she would have new clothes and sweets sent over to the mother-son duo, at her own expense, through the local Block Development Officer (BDO).

On another occasion, she came across a news about a poor daily wage labourer of Margo Munda village in Madhupur district who could not afford to get his son, who had qualified in the Joint Entrance Examination (JEE), the common all-India test for engineering courses, admitted to the National Institute of Technology (NIT), Jamshedpur, due to his poverty. Murmu asked her private secretary J.P. Dash to check the veracity of the story from the local BDO. When she was convinced that the story was true, she immediately got an amount of Rs 65,000 from her discretionary funds transferred to the account of the man for his son to be admitted to NIT, Jamshedpur.

Her former principal secretary Santosh Satapathy recalls an incident where Governor Murmu helped a poor rickshaw-puller, whose wife had four successive miscarriages, have a baby. 'She roped in well-known gynecologist Dr Shobha for the purpose. The woman was under her treatment for about six months during which the Governor sanctioned an amount of

Rs 6000 from her discretionary funds for medicines. Due to the personal care and attention of Dr Shobha, the woman delivered a healthy baby, who is now a year and a half old and is doing fine. She even named the child "Rudra",' he says.

As Governor, Murmu would take stock of the day's happenings around the state every evening and decide if any matter needed her personal attention or intervention. She would be constantly on the lookout for anyone in distress and put her Rs 20 lakh discretionary funds to good use to provide succour to them.

During her tenure as Governor of Jharkhand, the Raj Bhavan in Ranchi got a complete makeover. A person who loved nature, she got a reservoir constructed inside the Raj Bhavan and oversaw the plantation of nearly 3000 fruit-bearing trees within the premises. Vegetables and flowers were also grown on a fairly large scale making the Raj Bhavan self-sufficient in these items. There was also a cowshed in the premises which used to take care of the milk requirements of the Raj Bhavan. Saal trees lined up the outer periphery of the Raj Bhavan.

A great believer in organic farming, she issued strict instructions to her staff that not an ounce of chemical fertilizer or pesticide was to be used in farming activities in the Raj Bhavan. In consultation with experts from Birsa Agricultural University and the Horticulture department, she experimented with planting various fruit-bearing trees, such as apples, pears, strawberry and papaya. Mushroom cultivation was also taken up on a large scale. Not all of the experiments were a success, but pineapple was a huge success. 'She always said, "Let a hundred experiments fail. If even one is a success, that is good enough,"' staff at the Raj Bhavan recall her telling them. Buoyed by her success, she tried to take these horticultural experiments beyond the confines of the Raj Bhavan and across the state. Using the agriculture and horticulture extension services, she promoted the plantation of fruit-bearing trees and flowers at various places in the state. Of all these experiments, orange plantation in Lohardaga area was a massive success.

More than a year and half after she laid down office as the Governor, the staff at the Raj Bhavan still miss Murmu's benign presence. She treated all of them with a lot of affection and respect and was always concerned about their welfare and well-being. 'She never had any gubernatorial air about her. She was a very simple person and always wore a smile on her face. No one ever saw her angry or heard her scolding anyone or raising her voice. I don't think we will ever get another Governor like her,' says a Class IV employee of the Raj Bhavan. She would regularly enquire about the well-being of her staff and their family members and help out anyone in need. Each staff member, irrespective of rank, received dresses or sarees and sweets on special occasions like Holi and Diwali. This was besides the uniforms they got as a matter of routine every year.

Murmu's day started at 3.30 a.m. She would get up from bed, do her yoga and prayers, take her bath and be ready for the day by 5 a.m. She would then feed the cows and birds in the Raj Bhavan premises and pour water on the roots of the peepul tree without fail before taking her breakfast. She was a frugal eater and a strict vegetarian, who shunned even onion and garlic in her food, a habit she has carried into the Rashtrapati Bhavan as well. She was not the kind to sit idle and always kept busy with something or the other. She travelled frequently, going to the remotest part of the state; sometimes on invitation, but often on her own to see the state of affairs at the grassroots level. She also visited other states at regular intervals. She was easily the most-travelled Governor Jharkhand has seen.

She made it a point not to miss festivals that showcased the rich culture and traditions of the state. 'Her faith in tribal traditions was unshakeable and she would never decline a request to be part of any religious or cultural event,' says former CM Babulal Marandi. 'I once accompanied her to Baramasia in Giridih district, a revered place of worship for Santhals, which celebrated a festival every year. The organizers were delighted to have the Governor taking part in their festivities,' recalls Marandi, now the leader of the Opposition in the Jharkhand Assembly. She also attended the Santhal festival organized in Dharamgarh in Bokaro district every year. But it was not as if she was partial to Santhal festivals. She participated in festivals of all communities: Ho, Mundas, Oraons, and so on. Tribal festivals like 'Sarhul' and 'Karma' were organized in the premises of the Raj Bhavan as well.

Murmu was truly eclectic in her religious beliefs. She met cardinals, sants and imams regularly. She offered 'chadars' at the mazar in Ranchi. On the occasion of the 'Prakash Utsav' to mark the 550th birth anniversary of Guru Nanak Dev, she went to Gurudwara Harmandir Sahib for the special celebrations. On her return, she got a *vatika* (garden) constructed inside the Raj Bhavan.

By all accounts, Murmu has an amazing ability to remember people and names. She would address people by their names even when she met them after years. Writing in the *Hindustan Times*, Brigadier Aditya Madan (retd) recalls an incident that highlighted this particular attribute of hers.[8] In the last week of January 2019, she had invited the Jharkhand NCC contingent, which had just swept almost all competitions organized in the run-up to the Republic Day parade, to the Raj Bhavan to honour them on their achievement. As commander of the Hazaribagh group, whose cadets had won the bulk of the prizes, Brig. Madan led his cadets to the Raj Bhavan. After the customary introduction was over, the cadets staged a programme they had planned for the occasion. 'The chief guest observed every cadet's performance with rapt attention with her ears glued to the names of participants being called out by the master of ceremonies. After the programme, during her informal interaction with the participants, we were taken aback when she addressed all cadet participants by their names like an exceptional mnemonist,' writes Brig. Madan.

Murmu ticked all the boxes that a copybook Governor is expected to follow. She was fair and even-handed, treating the Opposition with as much respect as she did the treasury benches, earning the respect of both sides in the process. She rose above her party loyalties and upheld the Constitution and the dignity of the office she held at all times: as Governors are sworn to do but seldom do in practice. She was not averse to putting her foot down as she did when she returned the two land tenancy amendment Bills. At a time when the state government was under fire from all corners due to the Pathalgadi movement, she acted like a statesman in diffusing what was fast turning out to be a highly volatile situation. She toured the state extensively and gave access to people from all walks of life. She always tried to help people in distress and put her discretionary funds to good use for the purpose. And she did her best to improve things in respect of the two most crucial areas of governance—education and health—not by bypassing the government, but by working in close coordination with it.

In short, she was just the kind of Governor the Constitution envisaged and was a perfect role model for all future Governors.

# 10

# Commoner Again

Having completed her highly successful term as Governor of Jharkhand, Murmu returned to her home town Rairangpur in July 2021 and began life afresh as a 'commoner'. There was not much of a change in her routine after she settled into the modest house her husband had bought in the town with her younger brother Taranisen Tudu and his wife Shukri, who have been living with her since she lost her husband and two sons. She still woke up at 3.30 a.m., took her bath and did her yoga and prayers. The only addition to the routine she followed in the Ranchi Raj Bhavan was a round of morning walk with her sister-in-law.

She began visiting the Prajapita Brahma Kumaris Ishwariya Vishwa Vidyalaya centre in town and taking part in its activities on a regular basis, something she could not do while she was Governor of Jharkhand. She also started taking part in various sociocultural activities in the town.

Even as a child, Murmu had understood the importance of education in the making of a person's life as well as in nation-building. That is why she had fought hard to give herself the best possible education despite seemingly insurmountable odds. To make sure that the children of her area did not suffer the same fate and go far to get quality education like she did, she had constituted a trust and opened a residential school for students of classes VI to X in Pahadpur, her in-laws' village, in 2016 while she was Governor of Jharkhand. The school was named Shyam-Laxman-Sipun (SLS) Memorial Residential School in memory of her late husband and her two departed sons. She donated a piece of land measuring 3.2 acres belonging to her in-laws' family for setting up of the school. One of the first things that draws the attention of the visitor to the school is a small garden that has three memorial plaques devoted to the three persons in whose name the school was opened: Shyam (Murmu's husband), Laxman (her elder son) and Sipun (younger son). Since the very beginning, Murmu has made it a point to visit the school on the birth anniversaries of the three and pay floral tributes to them.

But there were teething problems that had to be sorted out for the school to get going. For one thing, she needed a trustworthy person who shared her vision to look after the affairs of the school since she herself was Governor of Jharkhand at the time. For another, it was hard to get students for the school in a predominantly tribal area beset with poverty and lack of awareness. There were very few people who could afford to pay even the minimal charges fixed by the school.

The first problem was the easier of the two to solve as she roped in two people she knew well: Prasanna Kumar Sahu, a civil engineer by profession, and Munna Pratihari, an employee of a nearby college, to manage the school. But the second proved a much bigger challenge.

Recalling those early days of struggle, Sahu, who is now the president of the school management committee, says, 'We had a tough time getting students for the school. We talked to many parents in the area and managed to find just sixteen students in the first year with great difficulty, and that too after promising to take care of the fees of those who could not afford it. But having got the sixteen students, we realized that we had an even bigger challenge on our hands since those who took admission did not know anything. Some of them could not even write their names!'

The teachers at the school, including the headmaster Priyabrata Mohanta, had to work hard to bring the students up to the mark. They organized an intensive, three-month crash course during which the students were taught the basics of alphabets and numbers. The regular Class VI syllabus was taken up only after the three-month orientation programme.

Things improved marginally in the second year as twenty Class VI students took admission. But the fees of many of them had to be subsidized, as in the first year, for them to pursue their studies in the school. From the second year, a new class was opened every year till it had classes up to X. But even now, the school is yet to get the status of an examination centre for the Class X board because of which the students have to appear in their examinations through another school in the area.

The second year also saw a new headmaster, Janmejay Giri, take over and more teachers appointed. But the Covid-19 pandemic proved to be a huge setback for the school as the students had to go home and did not return for nearly two years. Things began looking up again in 2021 as the situation improved and the students returned to school. At present, the school has eighty-eight students and eight teachers, including three women, all of whom stay on the school premises to ensure proper care and attention to the students. All of them worked hard to carry out the vision Murmu had outlined for the school. Their efforts finally bore fruit in 2022 when all eighteen students at the school who had appeared in the Class X examinations conducted by the Board of Secondary Education (BSE), Odisha, passed out with first division.

As part of its efforts to carry out the vision of Murmu, the school has always laid great emphasis on extra-curricular activities to ensure the students develop a well-rounded personality and not just strive for academic excellence. Towards this end, the students take part in extra-curricular activities like yoga, sports, singing, dancing and oration on a regular basis.

From the very beginning, Murmu has loomed large in the school even though she was not around physically. 'Murmu ji was determined to make it a centre of excellence for local students who could not afford to go to fancy schools far away for quality education. Even when she was Governor, she monitored the affairs of the school on a regular basis and helped out with money and anything the school required. Apart from funding the education of students, she also took care of their medical expenses, if any. When a student fell seriously ill, she arranged for him or her to be taken to Ranchi where he or she received the best possible medical attention and was cured soon,' says Sahu. She also used her good offices to get the Indian Oil Corporation to sanction money for construction of a new building out of its CSR funds. The building, completed in 2021, now houses two classrooms, besides the school office.

After she laid down office as Governor of Jharkhand and returned to Rairangpur, Murmu had time on her hands to pay greater attention to the affairs of the school. 'The school is very close to the President's heart. Before assuming office as the President, she used to visit the school and interact with the students and teachers on a regular basis,' says Munna Pratihari, the vice-president of the school management committee and a close associate of Murmu.

With Murmu's ascension to the highest constitutional office in the country, the school has now got national recognition. It has already started receiving the benefits of its association with the First Citizen of the country. The moment of crowning glory came when it was chosen as one of only four schools in the country to get the first taste of 5G technology during a demonstration of the service, ahead of its formal launch, on 2 October 2022, Gandhi Jayanti day. Executives of Reliance Jio, the first company to offer 5G services in India, reached Pahadpur before D-day to set up a temporary tower in the school premises to enable live, high-speed connection with the Indian Mobile Congress (IMC) inaugurated by PM Modi at Pragati Maidan in New Delhi. The temporary tower will be replaced by a permanent tower in due course, company officials say.

The students at the school, located in a remote tribal village, were over the moon after getting a rare opportunity to interact directly with the PM and other dignitaries at the IMC event in the national capital via Jio True 5G. 'We are delighted at the opportunity to interact with the PM. He told us how 5G technology will transform the education sector,' said a starry-eyed Class VIII student who took part in the live demonstration.

With the founder now ensconced in the Rashtrapati Bhavan, the school and its students can certainly look forward to better days ahead.

Having put the affairs of the school in safe, trusted hands, Murmu now had time on her hands to revive her social and philanthropic work. Her associates say she also planned to set up an old-age home in the area.

Even as she was doing all this, politics was never far from her mind. Soon after completing her stint as Jharkhand Governor and returning to her home town, she had made it abundantly clear in an interview given to leading Odia daily *Sambad* that she would get back to active politics and work for the people. Proving right the adage 'Once a politician, always a politician', she rejoined the party she had quit after being appointed Governor. Appearing on the popular talk show *Kholakatha* on Odisha's No. 1 TV news channel OTV, around the same time, she had outlined her rationale

for returning to active politics and rejoining the BJP
thus: 'I cannot reach out to the people I want to work
for unless I am in the party. I am just sixty-three,
physically fit and mentally sound. I thus have plenty of
years left to be in politics and work for the people and
the party before I reach the "superannuation" age of
seventy-five that Prime Minister Narendra Modi has
set.' She had said she was not hankering after any posts
and would be happy to spend the rest of her life as an
ordinary party worker. 'Politics for me is a means to
serve the people and I will continue to work for them
till my body allows me,' she had told Manaranjan
Joshi, the anchor of the show.[1]

The two back-to-back interviews made it clear
that there was absolutely no ambiguity in Murmu's
mind about her role post her stint as Governor. But
she obviously realized that she could not go back to
her old ways and had to maintain a certain decorum
in her public dealings. Hence, she refrained from
participating in overt party activities in deference to
her newly acquired status as an 'ex-Governor'. She
rarely attended party meetings during this phase but
met her party colleagues at her home and discussed
various issues, including party strategy, with them.

Ramachandra Murmu, who met her at her
Rairangpur residence at the time, says though she did
not spell it out in as many words, he got the distinct
impression that she would return to politics. 'Since she

had already been a Governor, we thought she would be made an MP. As the Lok Sabha elections were over three years away, we expected that she would be sent to the Rajya Sabha. But when that did not happen, we thought maybe she was being considered for something bigger, given her excellent rapport with PM Modi. But never in our wildest dream did we imagine that she would be chosen as the President of the country,' Murmu says.

Her close associate Nabin Ram says she would have returned to active electoral politics and would have, in all likelihood, contested the next parliamentary elections had she not been named as the presidential candidate of the ruling alliance. 'During the municipal elections in March 2022, she did her bit for the party though she did not campaign openly. When rumours about a rift between us were floated by our rivals, she released a video rubbishing reports of any rift and appealing to the people to vote for me,' says Ram, who contested the election for the post of municipal chairperson, but lost to the BJD candidate by 1000-odd votes.

Notwithstanding what Ram says, it is hard to tell what exactly was in Murmu's mind. It is possible, as he says, that she would have contested the 2024 parliamentary elections if she had not been fielded as the NDA candidate for President. But it is highly unlikely that she would have lobbied for a party ticket. She is an extremely reticent person who is very conscious of her image in public, says BJP national vice-president Jay Panda, who has known her for more than two decades. 'When her name had started doing the rounds as a possible NDA candidate for President, I had asked her in one of our meetings, "Why don't you come to Delhi more often?" She just smiled and did not say anything. She was very conscious not to be seen doing anything that could be misconstrued as lobbying. This is the highest standard of probity in public life that you expect in a judge of the higher court, not in a politician,' he says. It is, in fact, a testament to the good work she has done that she never had to lobby for any position during her political career; everything, from the municipal vice chairperson's post to highest constitutional post in the country, came to her on a platter.

Her reticence, however, did not prevent her party colleagues from doing their bit to push her case. Nabin Ram, for one, openly admits to organizing a spate of favourable reports in both the state and national media after learning from 'top party sources' that the powers that be were in favour of fielding a tribal as the party's presidential candidate this time. 'We sent the clippings to the Prime Minister's Office (PMO),' he says. It is doubtful if the media clippings played any role in the party choosing Murmu as its presidential candidate. But there is very little doubt that her stellar record as the Governor of Jharkhand did influence her choice, as did the fact that she is a tribal and a woman.

# 11

# President Murmu

25 July 2022 will go down as a historic day in the evolution of India as a nation state. It was the day when a person born in independent India was sworn in as the President of the republic for the first time. Eight years before, PM Modi had become the first person born after Independence to take oath as the PM of the country. The process of transition of the national leadership to the post-Independence generation that began on 24 May 2014 was completed with the swearing-in of Murmu as the President of the country on 25 July 2022. It was perhaps fitting that the completion of the process came at a time when the nation was celebrating 'Azadi ka Amrit

Mahotsav' to mark seventy-five years of India's independence.

This, however, was not the only reason for the historical significance of the day. It was also the day when a tribal ascended the highest constitutional position in the country for the first time. The implications of this development can hardly be overstated. The country had already had two Presidents from the Dalit (scheduled caste) community, among the poorest and most oppressed sections of Indian society over the centuries, in K.R. Narayanan and Ram Nath Kovind, Murmu's immediate predecessor. The anointment of a tribal, the other most neglected section of society, as President, thus represented a very important milestone in the evolution of the Indian republic and fulfilled the promise of a truly egalitarian society held out by the Constitution of India. Cynics would, of course, dismiss it as mere symbolism. Pointing to the largely ornamental nature of the post of President in the constitutional scheme of things in India, they would claim that a truer test—and more authentic proof—of the emancipation of the neglected classes would be when a Dalit or a tribal becomes the PM of the country. But one must remember that Murmu's rise to the President's post is just a very important step in the evolution of the Indian republic, not its final destination. Thirty years ago, a tribal at Raisina Hills would perhaps have been unthinkable. But here we are, with a tribal occupant of the Rashtrapati Bhavan since 2022. For all we know, the country could see a Dalit or a tribal PM a few decades down the line. (In fact, India came pretty close to having a Dalit PM, Jagjivan Ram, in the post-Emergency election in 1977, but it was Morarji Desai who prevailed in the end.)

In her first speech after being sworn in as President, Murmu emphasized the significance of her ascension to the post thus. 'It is a tribute to the power of our democracy that a daughter born in a poor house in a remote tribal area can reach the highest constitutional position in India. That I attained the post of President is not my personal achievement; it is the achievement of every poor person in India. My election is a proof of the fact that the poor in India can have dreams and fulfil them too,' she said in her address (in Hindi) after being administered the oath of office by Justice N.V. Ramana, the then Chief Justice of India (CJI).[1]

During her speech, President Murmu recalled her personal struggles early in life and how she overcame them to become the first girl from her village to reach college. 'It is a matter of great satisfaction for me that those who have been deprived of the benefits of development for centuries—the poor, the Dalits, the backward classes and tribals—see in me their reflection,' she said as she stressed on her humble origins and her rise through the ranks from a municipal councillor to the President of India. She hailed the tribal way of life, which has enabled them to live a sustainable life in perfect harmony with nature for thousands of years. 'It gives me great satisfaction that India is showing the way to the world when it comes to conservation of the environment,' she said.

While recalling the contributions of the leaders of India's freedom struggle like Pandit Jawaharlal Nehru, Sardar Vallabhbhai Patel and Netaji Subhas Chandra Bose, she made special mention of the role played by tribal uprisings like the Santhal rebellion, the Paika rebellion, and the Kol and Bhil uprisings in strengthening the Independence movement and paid glowing tributes to Santhal icon 'Dharti Abba' Bhagwan Birsa Munda. She also hailed the fortitude with which the people of India fought the Covid-19 pandemic.

'India not only took care of itself in these difficult situations but also helped the world. In the atmosphere created by the Corona pandemic, today the world is looking at India with a new confidence,' she said.[2]

Her dignified eighteen-minute speech was punctuated by thunderous applause from the assembled crowd at the Central Hall of Parliament. As she winded up her speech with a quote from Odia saint-poet Bhima Bhoi—'*mo jeebana pachhe narke padithau, jagata uddhara heu* [Let my life rot in hell, but may the world be saved]'—the clapping reached a crescendo.

While the virtual who's who of Indian politics—from the outgoing president Ram Nath Kovind, Vice-President M. Venkaiah Naidu, PM Modi and his Cabinet colleagues to Governors and CMs of various states—top military, civil and judicial officials and heads of diplomatic missions were present at the Central Hall of Parliament for the swearing-in ceremony, what caught the eye of the observers—especially from Odisha—was the pride of place given to Naveen Patnaik, the CM of Odisha, in the seating arrangements. He was seated in the front row even as other CMs and several Union ministers were given the second row. The special honour reserved for Patnaik was an indication as much of his strong bond with his 'rakhi sister' as of the important role he had played in ensuring the victory of the new President.

Among the profusion of VVIPs, however, there was a group of five dozen ordinary people from the President's home district, Mayurbhanj, specially invited by the President for the occasion. This bunch of sixty consisted of some of the President's family members, including her younger brother Taranisen and sister-in-law Shukramani, a few of her close friends, six BJP MLAs from the President's home district and three representatives of the Rairangpur centre of the Prajapita Brahma Kumaris Ishwariya Vishwa Vidyalaya. While leaving Rairangpur, Shukramani had told the media that she was carrying a 'jhal' saree, traditionally worn by Santhali women on special occasions, for her sister-in-law to wear on this once-in-a-lifetime occasion. No wonder most people thought—and media houses reported—that the white saree with green-and-red border the President was wearing on the occasion was a 'jhal' saree. No one stopped to verify that the animal, bird and leaf motifs, so much an integral part of the jhal design, were missing in the saree the President was wearing. In its over-enthusiasm, an Odia news channel even asked all its lady anchors to wear specially procured jhal sarees throughout the day of the swearing-in, till Amrita Sabat, a Bhubaneswar-based entrepreneur specializing in handloom wear, spoiled the fun by revealing that the saree the President was wearing on the occasion was actually 'a ganga jamuna phoda kumbha silk saree with bomkai work in anchal', usually made by master weavers of Sonepur.[3]

Most of the women in the group of sixty specially invited guests, however, attended the swearing-in ceremony of the new President dressed in jhal sarees. They were in for a pleasant surprise when they were invited to join the President for lunch at the Rashtrapati Bhavan. 'We were very happy to attend the President's oath-taking ceremony at the Central Hall of the Parliament, but never imagined we would be invited to have lunch at Rashtrapati Bhavan,' said an ecstatic Sujata Murmu, a former Zilla Parishad chairperson of Mayurbhanj district. In keeping with the new President's culinary choices, the lunch was a fully vegetarian affair. They also had an opportunity of a lifetime to experience first-hand the grandeur of the majestic Rashtrapati Bhavan as they were taken around the magnificent building with over 300 rooms built by the Britishers and shown the office of the President by the staff. 'While leaving the Rashtrapati Bhavan, each of us was given a packet of sweets. It was a memorable occasion,' said Murmu.

Even a month after the event, Dangi Murmu, Murmu's lifelong friend, still cannot get over the sheer excitement of watching her childhood buddy taking oath as the President of India. 'A torrent of memories from our school days came flooding into my mind as I watched her taking oath and heard her speech. I still get goosebumps when I think about it. It was an exhilarating, out-of-the-world experience,' she says with a tinkle in her eyes. She recalls, with childlike glee, the lunch hosted at the Rashtrapati Bhavan and gloats over the silver bowls and spoons in which the food was served and the designer glasses in which water was served. She even shows the tastefully designed card from the Rashtrapati Bhavan inviting her to join the President for lunch, which she has carefully preserved.

Less than three weeks after assuming office, Murmu had her first opportunity to address the nation on the eve of Independence Day. The highlight of her address was the special focus on the participation of women in nation-building. 'Gender inequalities are reducing, and women are moving ahead, breaking many glass ceilings. Their increasing participation in social and political processes will prove decisive. At the grassroots level, we have more than 14 lakh elected women representatives in Panchayati Raj Institutions. Our daughters are the biggest hope for the nation. [...] From becoming fighter pilots to space scientists, our daughters are scaling great heights,' she said.[4]

There has been very little change in Murmu's routine even after she moved into the Rashtrapati Bhavan. She still gets up at 3.30 a.m., does her yoga and prayers before getting ready for the day's engagements. She remains a frugal eater and goes to bed early. Just about the only thing that has changed is the menu at the Rashtrapati Bhavan. Non-vegetarian food is a strict 'No No' at the sprawling campus, except when she is hosting some foreign dignitaries. Sources say *pakhala* (fermented rice loved by most Odias) and all varieties of 'saga' (spinach)—her favourite dishes—have been added to the Rashtrapati Bhavan menu.

By all accounts, President Murmu has acquitted herself extremely well since taking over as the head of the State. She has conducted herself with the dignity expected of the high office she holds. Just as she did during her tenure as Governor of Jharkhand, she has been touring various states frequently. On her visits, she has gone out of her way to interact with common people endearing herself to them in the process. During an interaction with women tea garden workers at the Durgabari tea estate in Tripura in October 2022, she asked one of them, 'Do you send your children to school?' She also enquired if their quota of free rice and other government benefits reached them on time. Then, to the surprise of everyone present, she asked them, 'Can you identify CM Manik Saha and local MLA Krishnadhan Das?' The women nodded in affirmation and pointed to the two leaders in question who were accompanying her. 'They are local. Contact them if you have a problem,' she advised them.

On 5 September, the birth anniversary of former president Sarvepalli Radhakrishnan celebrated in India as Teacher's Day, President Murmu won the hearts of countrymen when she chose to come down from the stage to greet and present the Teacher's Day award to Pradeep Negi, a teacher from Uttarakhand with physical disability.

On 15 November 2022, the birthday of Bhagwan Birsa Munda, which is being celebrated nationally as Janjatiya Gaurav Diwas (Tribal Pride Day) since 2021, President Murmu became the first head of the State to reach Ulihatu, the native place of the tribal icon and eminent freedom fighter and pay floral tributes at his statue in the village. It was a great honour for the people of the village, located about 70 kilometres from Ranchi, to have no less than the President of the country come and pay respect to the Son of the Soil.

There was, however, a bit of a mystery over the curtailment of what was originally scheduled to be a two-day visit to the state by the President. As per the original itinerary drawn up, she was to arrive on 14 November, a day before the Janajatiya Gaurav Divas, and visit the Baidyanath Dham temple in Deoghar before spending the night at the Raj Bhavan which was her abode for six long years not so long ago. The next day, apart from visiting Ulihatu, the President was scheduled to attend the Jharkhand Foundation Day function organized by the Jharkhand government at the Morabadi Ground in Ranchi. But both the visit to Deoghar and the participation in Jharkhand Foundation Day celebrations were struck off the itinerary at the last minute and what was supposed be a two-day visit became a mere two-hour stopover before the President flew to Shahdol in Madhya Pradesh to address the Janjatiya Samagam (tribal convention). No reasons were cited for the last-minute change either by the Rashtrapati Bhavan or by local officials. But it is possible that ongoing political slugfest between the Hemant Soren government and the central government could be a reason for the rescheduling.

President Murmu has conducted herself with the dignity that her office demands and has managed to stay clear of the political mudslinging—at least so far. If her lifelong association with the BJP did not prevent her from enjoying the confidence of the Opposition and oppose the ruling BJP where required when she was Governor, there is no reason to believe she would do anything different as President.

Murmu's elevation to the post of President is certainly a good advertisement for Indian democracy. But the entrenched racism and misogyny of Indian society lurking just below the surface has repeatedly come to the fore since her nomination for the post. Regrettably, it has not stopped showing its ugly face even after she assumed the high office. If it was the tasteless and unbecoming remarks of RJD leader Tejashwi Yadav and Congress leader Ajoy Kumar in the run-up to the presidential election, Congress leader Adhir Ranjan Chowdhury carried the baton as it were after she became the President by referring to her as 'Rashtrapatni'—in a mischievous pun on the Hindi term for President, 'Rashtrapati'—during a chat with a news channel. This was just three days after Murmu was sworn in as the President. Union ministers Nirmala Sitharaman and Smriti Irani lambasted the Congress leader for his tasteless remark inside Parliament, which was in session at the time. 'Calling the President "Rashtrapatni" is a sexist

insult since "Rashtrapati" is a gender agnostic term,'
Sitharaman said in the Rajya Sabha, the Upper House
of Parliament.[5] In the Lok Sabha, Irani was more
scathing in nailing Chowdhury for his remark. 'You
stand guilty of insulting the supreme commander of the
armed forces. You stand guilty of humiliating a tribal
leader. The Congress party cannot stand the honour
given to a tribal. It is not able to digest a poor, tribal
woman becoming the President of India,' she said as
BJP members raised a din over the issue.[6] Both Houses
of Parliament had to be adjourned due to vociferous
protests by MPs belonging to the ruling party, who
also held a demonstration at Gate No. 4 of Parliament
against what they called an 'insult' to the President.
There were protest marches against Chowdhury's
remarks in several BJP-ruled states while an FIR was
lodged against him in Madhya Pradesh.

But even after the sharp reaction his comments
had provoked, Chowdhury remained defiant. 'There
is no question of apologising. I had mistakenly said
"Rashtrapatni". In a deliberate design, the ruling party
is trying to make a mountain out of a molehill,' he
told reporters.[7] But as the issue threatened to snowball
into a major controversy and an embarrassment for
the Congress, he tendered a written apology to the
President. 'I am writing to express my regret for having
mistakenly used an incorrect word to describe the
position you hold. I assure you that it was a slip of

the tongue. I apologise and request you to accept the same,' he said in the letter to the President.

Speaking to the media, Chowdhury sought to explain away his 'slip of tongue' by citing his poor knowledge of Hindi. 'I am a Bengali and don't know Hindi too well. That's why there was a grammatical mistake,' he said in his defence.

After a lull of about two months, Congress leader Udit Raj found himself in a soup after taking an unwarranted dig at the President. Raj, a tribal himself, picked on a comment by President Murmu, clearly made in zest, during a visit to Gujarat, the home state of PM Modi, to have a go at her. Addressing a civic reception organized in her honour by the Gujarat government, the President, while noting that the state produces 76 per cent of the salt consumed in the country, had added in a lighter vein that 'It can be said that the salt produced by Gujarat is consumed by all Indians.' Raj's reaction to this harmless, innocuous comment was savage, to say the least. 'No country should get a president like Droupadi Murmu. This is height of sycophancy. She says 70 per cent of people eat Gujarat's salt. Spend your life eating salt, then you will know the truth,' he tweeted in Hindi.[8]

The reaction to this disparaging comment by Raj, the chairman of the Unorganised Workers and Employees' Congress, on the President's casual remark was swift and strong. Dubbing Raj's comment as reflective of the Congress's 'anti-tribal mindset', BJP spokesperson Sambit Patra said, 'This is not the first time they have used such words. Congress' Adhir Ranjan Choudhury did it too.' 'After Ajoy Kumar called President Droupadi Murmu as evil & then Adhir Ranjan Choudhury used the term "Rashtrapatni", now Congress stoops to a new low,' another BJP spokesperson Shehzad Poonawalla tweeted.[9] On a visit to the steel city Rourkela in Odisha four days after making the disparaging comment on the President, Raj faced the ire of BJP workers who hurled eggs at his car and waved black flags at him in protest against his remarks.

Taking cognizance of the matter, the National Commission for Women (NCW) summoned Raj for his derogatory remarks against the President. Cornered on all sides, Raj finally issued a regret of sorts but remained defiant. While admitting that his own choice of words was wrong, he advised the President to choose her words carefully before giving statements. 'The phrase "namak khana" carries a deeper meaning. There was a mistake in my choice of words. I regret that. I will keep asking questions. I don't hanker after posts. I am a representative of SCs and STs and I get agonised when I find people representing them doing nothing from their high positions,' he tweeted.[10]

As if to prove that Congress leaders did not have a monopoly over derogatory remarks against the President, Trinamool Congress (TMC) minister Akhil Giri said something about her that breached all canons of decency. Addressing a public gathering at Nandigram on 11 November, Giri made a highly insulting comment on the President's looks, saying it evokes laughter even among her supporters.[11] As the video of the event went viral, there were protests by BJP workers and others not just in West Bengal, but in Odisha and several other states too. BJP workers took out protest rallies demanding Giri's sacking across West Bengal, including Kolkata. A party worker filed an FIR against the minister at Nandigram, the place where the offensive comment was made, while another complaint was filed at the Parliament Street police station in New Delhi, the national capital. BJP MP from Bishnupur Saumitra Khan also filed a complaint with the National Commission for Women (NCW), which asked Giri to tender an 'unconditional apology' while also writing to the West Bengal DGP to initiate a probe into the comments and take appropriate steps. Union Tribal Affairs Minister Arjun Munda said, 'He [Giri] has hurt the sentiments of the 10 crore tribals in the country and dented the country's democratic values.'[12]

In neighbouring Odisha, Murmu's home state, BJP organized protest rallies calling for Giri's head at several places across the state. BJP national spokesperson Sambit Patra, who participated in a rally at Nayagarh town, said, 'The Trinamool leader's comment has hurt the sentiments of the five-crore people of Odisha. We demand that West Bengal CM Mamata Banerjee sack him from the council of ministers and arrest him. His comment is not only derogatory to the highest post in the country, it is also anti-women and anti-tribal.'[13] The ruling BJD and Congress also condemned the comment made by Giri and demanded his removal from the council of ministers. 'He is not fit to be a minister. He should be dismissed from the council of ministers and suspended from the party without further delay,' said Munna Khan, the party's Rajya Sabha MP.[14] Senior Congress leader Taraprasad Bahinipati went a step forward and asked for an apology from TMC chief and West Bengal CM Mamata Banerjee and the arrest of Giri.

Realizing the sensitivity of the issue, the TMC not only disassociated itself from the minister's comments but also condemned it strongly. 'We have the utmost respect for Hon'ble President of India, Smt Droupadi Murmu. Our party strongly condemns the unfortunate remarks made by MLA @AkhilGiriAITC and clarifies that we do not condone such statements. In the era of women's empowerment, such misogyny is unacceptable,' read an official statement released by the TMC on the issue.[15]

With his own party refusing to back him, the minister for Prisons had little option but to tender an apology, attributing his offensive comment to a 'momentary lapse of judgment'. 'I also have deepest respect for the chair of the President, who is the head of the Constitution. Over the past few days and months, I have been subjected to ridicule, humiliation and abuse by the Bengal opposition leader and BJP's Suvendu Adhikari. I am old and I was angry. Whatever I said was said in anger in its response, which was a momentary lapse of judgment,' he said.[16]

But the protests continued even after Giri apologized. Three days after Giri made the disparaging comments, BJP MLAs in West Bengal marched to the Raj Bhavan under the leadership of Suvendu Adhikari to present a memorandum to the Governor demanding the sacking of the minister. The issue was finally put to rest only after Banerjee offered a public apology on behalf of his erring minister. 'I condemn Akhil Giri's comment on President Murmu. What Akhil has done is wrong. We don't support such a remark. I apologize on behalf of my party as he is my party colleague. The party has already cautioned Akhil Giri,' she said while addressing a press conference at Nabanna.[17]

Despite the apology tendered by the dramatis personae involved in each of the three incidents mentioned above, there is no guarantee that such indiscretions will not be repeated in future. Never known for discretion and restraint in public utterances, Indian politicians of all hues have an uncanny knack of putting their foot in the mouth.

# 12

# Homecoming

President Murmu's maiden, two-day visit to Odisha on 10 and 11 November will always remain special and memorable for the 4.5 crore people of her home state. The first person from the state to rise to the top constitutional post in the country won over the people with her humility and charm during the visit. It was as much a thanksgiving visit as it was a trip down memory lane for the President, who spent the better part of her adolescence and youth in Bhubaneswar, the capital city.

Not surprisingly, President Murmu began her two-day tour with a trip to Puri, the abode of Lord Jagannath, to pray at the twelfth-century shrine dedicated to the presiding deity of Odisha. After meeting the dignitaries assembled to greet her—including Governor Prof. Ganeshi Lal and CM Patnaik—on her arrival at the Biju Patnaik International Airport, she flew straight to Puri on an Indian Air Force (IAF) chopper.

A visit to the Jagannath Temple is invariably part of every visiting President to the state. As per the protocol followed on such occasions, the President's carcade drives down the Grand Road and stops right in front of Singhadwara, the entrance to the shrine. But Murmu took her security staff by surprise when she alighted from her vehicle at Balagandi Square and started walking towards the temple 2 kilometres away. Accompanied by her daughter Itishree and Union Education and Skill Development Minister Dharmendra Pradhan, she alternately raised her hands in supplication to the Lord, as most devotees do, and waved to the crowd that had lined up on either side of the Grand Road all along the way. Chants of '*Jay Jagannath*' and '*Bharat Mata ki Jai*' rent the air as the crowd went delirious at this heart-warming gesture by the President. All along the road, various dance groups performed in her honour and the President stopped for a few moments at each of them to greet the performers. On the way, she also stopped and broke out of the security cordon to accept the greetings of the students of Utkal Hindi Vidyapitha, shake hands with them and even pose for a photo with them, sending her security personnel into a tizzy.

On reaching Singhadwar, she was given a warm welcome by the Gajapati King of Puri Dibyasingha Dev and others. She washed her feet and sprinkled water on her body at the fountain outside the temple, a ritual followed by every devotee to the shrine. She then prostrated herself in front of the temple, folded her hands in front of the Lord and touched the Aruna Stambha before entering the temple. As she climbed the twenty-two steps of the temple, she stooped to touch each step and then touched her forehead. She had darshan of the deities at the *garbha griha* (sanctum sanctorum) before taking a detour of the premises and offering prayers at the shrines devoted to Mahalaxmi and Bimala. Her family priest Baidyanath Mohapatra took her around the temple and performed puja for her. Before leaving the temple premises, she wrote in the visitor's book of her priest in Odia, 'I consider myself extremely fortunate to have darshan of Chaturdha Murati and the side deities. I got a rare divine feeling after praying to the presiding deity of Odias, Lord Jagannath. The Lord is the "daru debata" (wooden god) of the tribals and the Lord of the Universe. I pray to Him for the well-being of the whole mankind. Let our country reach the pinnacle of prosperity and development by the grace of Lord Jagannath.'

After the darshan of the deities, President Murmu went to the Puri Raj Bhavan. Here again, she chose to shun the presidential privilege and have mahaprasad, consisting of over twenty items, procured from the Jagannath temple while sitting on the floor in the company of the Gajapati King, Queen Leelavati, Union Minister Dharmendra Pradhan, State Minister Pradip Kumar Amat, her daughter Itishree and son-in-law Ganesh. Though brand-new brass utensils had been procured for her by the district administration, she insisted on having her mahaprasad on banana leaves. Murmu was all praise for its taste and wondered if she could take one of the 'suar sevaks' (cooks who prepare mahaprasad) with her to the Rashtrapati Bhavan so that she could partake of the divine dish in New Delhi too. 'But when she realized that it was not possible since the servitor renders hereditary service only inside the temple, she abandoned the idea,' said Madhab Pujapanda, a senior servitor and a member of the Shree Jagannath Temple management committee, who was present at the Raj Bhavan on the occasion.

Her fondness for mahaprasad, however, did not go unnoticed. In deference to her desire, the Puri district administration is planning to make special arrangements to send mahaprasad to the Rashtrapati Bhavan by flight at regular intervals. 'We will discuss with Rashtrapati Bhavan officials soon and take steps to send "mahaprasad" with a functionary for the President. It will take two to three hours to get mahaprasad delivered to Delhi by flight. We will also ensure that the sanctity of the "mahaprasad" is maintained while sending it,' Puri Collector Samarth Verma said in an interview.[1]

If the first day of President Murmu's two-day 'homecoming' visit was all about Lord Jagannath, the second day was a journey down memory lane. The highlight of the day's engagements was her return to her alma mater—Unit II Girls' High School in Bhubaneswar—where she was a student in the early 1970s and the hostel—Kuntala Kumari Sabat Adivasi Girls' Hostel—where she stayed for five long years, including her first year in college. Both the school and the hostel had been all decked up—and the students all charged up—to welcome the most illustrious student in their history. The preparations had started several days before the presidential visit. The walls of the school were given a fresh coat of paint and pictures drawn on them while the Birsa Munda and Tulsi Munda blocks of the hostel were given a facelift for the occasion. The authorities had thoughtfully refurbished Room No. 6 in the Tulsi Munda block of the hostel where Murmu stayed. They repaired, renovated and put up for display the cot on which she once slept.

As the President's convoy entered the school premises, she was welcomed by students who played a band and escorted her to the makeshift stage put up for her on the occasion. One group of students sang

'*Bande Utkal Janani*', the state anthem, while another group of ten performed a Santhali dance in her honour. As soon as the performances were over, the President went up to the stage and posed for photographs with the performers. Next, she unveiled a sand art of herself made by the students. Samir Ranjan Dash, the School and Mass Education Minister of Odisha, presented the framed page from the school admission register that records her admission in the school on 21 July 1970. The register, signed by the then assistant warden of the hostel, mentions her maiden name Droupadi Tudu and her father Biranchi Narayan Tudu's name and records her village name as Uparbeda and her birthday as 20 June 1958.

It was a memorable occasion for twelve of the President's former classmates who had been specially invited to meet the head of the State by the school authorities. They were over the moon as the President smiled at them, greeted them and exchanged pleasantries. 'Where is Chuni?' she asked her friends, surprising them with her amazing ability to remember names of classmates she had not met in ages. She was enquiring about her close friend Chinamayee Gochhayat, who was supposed to be part of the alumni group invited to meet the President but could not come as she was out of town.

'It is hard to express the feeling. Not only did she recognize us by name, she also introduced us to Union

Minister Dharmendra Pradhan and others who were accompanying her. We are extremely proud that our classmate is now the President of India,' gushed Usha Satapathy, her erstwhile classmate.[2] 'How we wished we could spend a little more time with her and relive memories from our school. But we realized that it was not possible since she is the President,' lamented Anita Patnaik, another ex-classmate of the President. Swati Mohanty, another member of the group of twelve, was chirpy like a schoolgirl as she recalled her school days with the President. 'We studied together from Class VIII to Class XI. I was the monitor in Class VIII. I had once made Murmu stand up on the bench after she committed some mistake,' she chuckled.

The President became emotional as she entered the hostel room where she stayed in her school days. She sat for a few moments on the renovated cot on which she used to sleep as an inmate of the hostel before getting up to have a look at a framed picture of herself with two of her classmates—Dangi Murmu and Sumitra Kisku and a solo picture of herself presented to her by two inmates of the hostel, Maya Majhi (Class IX) and Ashtami Majhi (Class VI). The school authorities had clearly chosen the two girls carefully. While Ashtami belongs to Uparbeda, the President's native village, Maya hails from the nearby Kulgi village. Ashtami could barely conceal her excitement at having got an opportunity to meet the most famous person of her village in person. 'When I told her that I hail from Uparbeda, she asked my father's name. When I told her my father's name is Budhan Majhi, she immediately recognized him. I felt elated that she could recognise my father,' she told media persons later.[3]

The President got nostalgic when she was shown a picture of Shantilata Gochhayat, the assistant superintendent of the hostel when she was a boarder of the hostel. 'Reminiscing about her hostel days, the President said she used to call Mrs Gochhayat "Yashoda Maa" (Lord Krishna's mother) because of her love and affection for the inmates. She thanked us for having preserved the pictures of her for all these years,' said Snehalata Prusty, the present assistant superintendent of the hostel, later.

President Murmu planted a Baula (*Mimusops elengi*) sapling in the hostel premises. Before leaving, she wrote in the visitor's book of the hostel. 'I am extremely happy after visiting the Kuntala Kumari Sabat Girls' Hostel. The visit refreshed some unforgettable memories of my student days. I became emotional while meeting the inmates of the hostel and teachers of the school. I am happy to note that girls are getting safe, clean and homely atmosphere here. I wish a bright future for the students,' she wrote in Odia.

The President's first stop for the day, however, was the Tapovan High School, a residential school for tribal students, in Khandagiri area of Bhubaneswar which was established in 1964 by the Tribal/Social Welfare department of Government of Odisha. During her brief stay in the school premises, she met and interacted with nine students and nine alumni. She revealed that she had come to the school several times before to get her nephew and to drop or fetch him from school. 'I am very happy to be back here,' she said. She even took part in a short Question and Answer (Q&A) session with the students. Answering a question asked by Itishree Tiyu, she said her grandmother was her role model. 'She was a brave woman and always went out of her way to help people in distress. She would always reach out to people suffering from some disease or some physical disability or during pregnancy and childbirth,' she said. To another question asked by Kalindi Hansda, she said things had changed a lot since the time she was in school. 'We did not get the facilities you are getting. The school in my village where I studied did not have a concrete roof and the floor peeled off at many places. You are lucky that you don't have to endure such a situation. So, make the best possible use of the facilities you get and study hard. You will certainly achieve success,' she said.

The curious onlookers waiting outside were intrigued when an official took out a briefcase from the vehicle and followed the President as she entered the school premises and wondered what its content could be. It later transpired that the briefcase contained dairy milk chocolates meant to be distributed among the students. Later in the day, while returning from Jayadaev Bhavan, where she launched the e-KUMBH (Knowledge Unleashed in Multiple Bharatiya Languages) portal and the Odia version of twenty engineering books, the President stopped when she saw a group of eager schoolgirls waving furiously at her. She alighted from the vehicle, went up to the girls and gave them chocolates. This is one habit she appears to have carried from her days as a schoolteacher in Rairangpur.

As the residents of Bhubaneswar rolled out the red carpet for the President and fell over one another to see her, get close to her and speak to her, the people in faraway Rairangpur were a disappointed lot as she skipped her home town on her on her first visit to the state. The people in Uparbeda and Pahadpur were equally disappointed, as were the students and teachers of the SLS school she had founded in Pahadpur. This was the first time in years when Murmu was not there at the school to pay her respects to her husband at his statue in the school premises on his birth anniversary, 1 August. But they do understand the constraints of time that the President of India has to function under. 'After all, she is the President. But I have no doubt whatsoever that she would come to Rairangpur whenever she visits Odisha next,' says Dasharathi Mohanta, a shopkeeper in Rairangpur town.

# 13

# Odisha's Finest Hour

When Indian PM Modi mentioned the Bali Yatra in Cuttack city of Odisha while speaking at Bali during the G20 summit in Indonesia on 15 November 2022, not many in the audience, mainly consisting of the Indian diaspora, would have known about the largest annual open-air fair in Asia on the banks of River Mahanadi in the Millennium City of Odisha. The name Bali Yatra, derived from Bali, commemorates the glorious maritime traditions and the millennia-old trade relations between Odisha, known as Kalinga at the time, and Southeast Asia in general and Bali in particular. Not many in India, except in academic circles, know that Odias were among the earliest seafarers of India who used to set sail for various countries in Southeast Asia and present-day Sri Lanka with their boats (called *boita* in Odia) laden with goods on Kartik Purnima day, the day the modern-day Bali Yatra fair begins, and return to base with stuff brought from these far-off lands in the month of Baishakha (April). These were large boats, which had copper sculls and could carry up to 700 men and animals. There were so many of them sailing in the sea that the Bay of Bengal was then known as the Kalinga Sea. The traders, known as *sadhabas* in Odia, usually carried, among other things, a wide array of textiles, brass and bell metal ware, lacquered boxes, intricate ivory, wood and stone carvings, pepper, betel nuts and Pattachitra paintings and palm leaf engravings, and brought pearls and silver, spices and sandalwood in exchange.

For hundreds of years, the people of Odisha have been commemorating this ancient marine adventure by their forefathers by floating tiny boats made out of barks of banana trees, with burning lamps placed inside, on the sea, in rivers and tanks early on the morning of Kartika Purnima in a symbolic recreation of the daring voyage of yore. No wonder the great poet Kalidasa, in his first-century tome 'Raghuvansham', refers to the King of Kalinga as the 'Mahodadhipati' (King of the Seas).

The ancient Odias who took the sea route to Indonesian islands like Java, Sumatra, Bali and Borneo (part of modern-day Indonesia) were, however, not just traders. Many of them actually married local women and settled down in these foreign lands. They carried their cultures, traditions and religion—Hinduism and later Buddhism—with them, remnants of which can be found in these societies even now. The uncanny similarities between many Odia and Balinese words make for a fascinating etymological study.

The fact that it was the bloodbath at Kalinga War in the third century BC that converted the winner, Emperor Ashoka, from 'Chandashoka' to Dharmashoka' and made him a votary of peace and non-violence and a missionary of Buddhism for the rest of his life is well known. The caves of Khandagiri and Udayagiri hills, located on the outskirts of Bhubaneswar city, stand mute testimony to the time when Buddhism and Jainism flourished in the state. But there are several other things about the ancient land of Odisha, known as 'Udra', 'Kalinga' and 'Utkala' at various times in history, that are not known to the rest of India, forget the rest of the world. How many people outside Odisha, for example, know that Buddhism flourished in the 'Golden Triangle' comprising Lalitgiri, Ratnagiri and Udayagiri in Odisha's Jajpur district, which is among the most important Buddhist sites in India, from third to eleventh century AD? And that the Pushpagiri Mahavihara there was among the important seats of Buddhist learning, next only to Nalanda in Bihar? Or, for that matter, the fact that it was a man from Odisha, Acharya Padmasambhava, who took Buddhism to Tibet in the seventh century? There is a monastery dedicated to him, the largest in eastern India, at Jeeranga in Gajapati district of Odisha.[1]

Even in modern times, there is a lot about Odisha that should have received much greater attention than it has. Take, for example, the Paika Rebellion of 1817, the first organized revolt against the Britishers, which has been dubbed 'the first war of Independence' by some historians as it took place forty years before the Sepoy Mutiny of 1857, which has enjoyed the title so far. That Odisha was the first state carved out on linguistic basis way back in 1936—eleven years before Independence and two decades before the other linguistic states were formed—is another little-known aspect of the state's history. As is the fact that it was the successful accession of the princely state of Nilagiri in present-day Balasore district that prepared the blueprint for the merger of the over 500 princely states across the country engineered by India's first Home Minister Sardar Vallabhbhai Patel. Utkal Gaurav Madhusudan Das, Utkalamani Gopabandhu Das, Nabakrushna Choudhury and Dr Harekrushna Mahatab were among the most prominent leaders of the Indian independence movement. Odia, the language spoken in the state, is one of the only six 'classical' languages of India, the other five being Sanskrit, Tamil, Telugu, Kannada and Malayalam.

However, post-Independence, Odisha somehow fell off the radar, as it were, due to a variety of sociopolitical and cultural factors. Despite its rich past and active participation in the Independence struggle, the state was pushed to the fringes of the national consciousness. The ignorance about Odisha in the rest of the country, the North in particular, is appalling. In fact, it is not uncommon for an Odia to be asked, especially in northern India, where Odisha is. While travelling to New Delhi on train a few years ago, this author had the mortification of being asked by a fellow passenger, 'Where exactly is Odisha? Is it in West Bengal or in Bihar?' And this about the state that was the first in the country to be carved out on linguistic basis!

Right through history, Lord Jagannath (Lord of the Universe) has remained the identity of Odisha. And things have not changed much even now. Puri and Jagannath ring a bell in the minds of Indians everywhere, even among those who cannot place Odisha on the Indian map. But there is a lot else about the state that should have got itself far greater national attention than it has managed. Apart from a 480-kilometre-long coastline, the state has an abundance of natural resources in the form of a large number of rivers, forests and rich flora and receives an annual precipitation of about 1400 mm. Its mineral resources are the envy of other states. It has 24 per cent of the total coal reserve in the country, 28 per cent of its iron ore, 59 per cent of bauxite and an incredible 98 per cent of chrome ore.[2]

With that kind of mineral resources, Odisha should have been an industrial powerhouse to rival the likes of Tamil Nadu and Maharashtra. But in the pre-liberalization regime, its minerals attracted the covetous eyes of industrial houses instead of investments while sustaining industries in other states. The first steel plant set up by the Tatas in Jamshedpur in the early twentieth century sourced almost its entire iron ore requirement from the rich mines of Badampahar and Gorumahisani, incidentally in Mayurbhanj district. Odisha's coal sustained power plants as far as in Gujarat and Tamil Nadu. Powerful movements against land acquisition for industrial houses and the prospective damage to environment by them did not help the cause of industrialization in the state. The prime example of this phenomenon was the mega port-based, integrated steel plant proposed to be set up by Tata Steel in Gopalpur in south Odisha's Ganjam district in the 1990s and the 12 MTPA (million tons per annum) integrated steel plant proposed to be set up near Pradeep in Jagatsinghpur district by steel major Posco of South Korea. Both these projects had to be abandoned due to stiff opposition by the local population.

Till the 1990s, Odisha was back of beyond in the national scheme of things. It was known as a land of grinding poverty, of starvation deaths, of child sale, and so on. These were the only things in the state that merited mention in the 'national' media. In 1985, the sale of Phanas Punji, a teenage girl, by her sister-in-law in Kalahandi (now Nuapada) district had made a big splash in the national media after which the then PM Rajiv Gandhi had visited Kalahandi. The visit resulted in the launch of a special, centrally funded project for poverty alleviation called ADAPT for what has come to be known as the KBK (Kalahandi-Bolangir-Koraput) region, one of the most underdeveloped areas in the whole country. Central schemes for poverty amelioration in the region under different names, each more ambitious than the previous one, continued over the years without any significant change in the ground realities.

The only other thing that made it into the national media was disasters. As a state with a 480-kilometre coastline and countless rivers, floods and cyclones have always been constant companions of Odisha. Even as the coastal areas have been repeatedly ravaged by floods and cyclone, droughts have been a recurring phenomenon in the arid regions of the west and south.

Things, however, began to change for the better for Odisha in the new millennium, which coincided with the advent of Naveen Patnaik in the political horizon of the state. When Patnaik took over as CM of Odisha on 5 March 2000, the state was still reeling under the debilitating impact of the Super Cyclone of 29 October 1999 that had ravaged the coastal districts, leaving nearly 10,000 dead and the physical infrastructure in complete disarray. The state's finances were in a shambles to the extent where the government had to borrow money to pay its employees. The BJD–BJP alliance government headed by Naveen Patnaik set about the task of rebuilding the state in right earnest. Through a combination of deft financial management and tough austerity measures (which involved a freeze on fresh recruitment in government service for years), the financial situation was nursed back to health. A series of well-thought-out policy measures, welfare schemes and their effective implementation on the ground saw extreme poverty become a thing of the past. The state's record in all developmental indices like infant mortality rate (IMR), maternal mortality rate (MMR) and malnutrition improved significantly. Simultaneously, a long-term disaster mitigation system was put in place to minimize damage due to disasters in future. As part of the exercise, the state government created Odisha State Disaster Mitigation (now Management) Authority (OSDMA), the first specialized agency in the country to fight disasters. In the new post-liberalization credo, which found merit in setting up industries where the raw material is, Odisha emerged as a major investment destination for both domestic industrial houses and multinational corporations (MNCs). Despite the setback of Posco and ArcellorMittal, industrialization of the state went apace. Of late, the state has also emerged as a major hub for sports, especially hockey, having already hosted the FIH Hockey World Cup twice, first in December 2018 and then again in January 2023. The Birsa Munda stadium built in the steel city of Rourkela for the 2023 edition of the FIH Hockey World Cup is the biggest and among the best in the world.

Despite the all-round improvement of Odisha, however, the political representation of the state at the national level has been nominal, notwithstanding the fact that it sends twenty-one members to the Lok Sabha, the Lower House of the Indian parliament. While there have been many Union ministers and Governors from the state, they haven't really outgrown the boundaries of the state and emerged as national leaders with the honourable exception of Biju Patnaik, who came within striking distance of becoming the PM in the United Front (UF) government formed after the fractured mandate in1996 before being pipped to the post by H.D. Deve Gowda.

For reasons that have not been adequately analysed, Odisha has always got a raw deal when it comes to representation in the Union council of ministers whenever the Congress has been in power at the Centre; even when it has sent fifteen to twenty MPs to the Lok Sabha. Take the 1984 elections, for example. The Congress had won a whopping twenty out of the twenty-one Lok Sabha seats in the state, but not one of them merited a place in the Union council of ministers. Even when MPs from the state have been made ministers, they are rarely given Cabinet rank, with the exception of J.B. Patnaik, who was inducted as the Cabinet minister for Tourism, Civil Aviation and Labour in the Indira Gandhi government in 1980. But his tenure as Union minister lasted less than a year as he was sent as the CM of Odisha later in the same year. As a result, Odisha has a long list of ministers of state in the council of ministers, not many of whom have risen to Cabinet rank. Senior leader Srikant Jena, who, as a Janata Dal MP, had been a Cabinet minister in the United Front government from 1996–98, had the ultimate ignominy of having to accept a Minister of State (MoS) position in the Dr Manmohan Singh government after the Congress came to power in 2004.

In contrast, the state has got far better representation whenever there has been a non-Congress government in New Delhi. Biju Patnaik was the Union Cabinet minister for Steel and Mines in the Janata Party government formed in 1977, while his party colleague Rabi Ray was made the Lok Sabha Speaker. Samarendra Kundu, the MP from Balasore, was inducted into the Union Council of Ministers as the minister of state for External Affairs. The next time there was a non-

Congress government, the V.P. Singh government in 1989, it was the turn of former Odisha CM Nilamani Routray to be appointed a Cabinet minister, first as the Union minister for Health and Family Welfare and then as Forests and Environment minister. Bhajaman Behera was made minister of state for petrochemicals.

Odisha got two Cabinet-rank ministers and two ministers of state with independent charge in the first, shortlived Atal Bihari Vajpayee government in 1998. While Naveen Patnaik was made the Cabinet minister for Steel and Mines and Jual Oram the Cabinet minister for the newly created Department of Tribal Affairs, Dillip Ray was appointed as MoS (independent charge) for Coal and Dr Debendra Pradhan, father of present Education minister Dharmendra Pradhan, as MoS (independent charge), Rural Development.

It was back to square one in the first Congress-led UPA government in 2004 headed by Dr Manmohan Singh when Chandra Sekhar Sahu was the lone flagbearer of Odisha in the Union council of ministers as minister of state for Rural Development. In 2009, it was the turn of Srikant Jena to represent Odisha in the council of ministers as MoS for Chemicals and Fertilizers.

Odisha got more than a fair share of its representation when the NDA government headed by PM Modi assumed office in May 2014. Jual Oram, the lone BJP MP from Odisha was made the

Cabinet minister for Tribal Affairs for the second time, Dharmendra Pradhan, elected to the Rajya Sabha from Madhya Pradesh, was given independent charge of Petroleum and Natural Gas. In the mid-term reshuffle, Pradhan was promoted to the Cabinet rank while holding the same portfolio. In the second Modi government that took office in 2019, Pradhan was given charge of the crucial ministries of Education and Skill Development while Pratap Sarangi was made MoS for Animal Husbandry, Dairy, Fisheries and Micro, Small and Medium Enterprises (MSME). Though he was dropped in the mid-term reshuffle, two more MPs from Odisha were inducted into the government. Ashwini Vaishnaw, Rajya Sabha MP from Odisha, was appointed as Cabinet minister with important portfolios like Railways, Communications and Electronics and Information Technology (IT) while Bisweswar Tudu, the MP from the Mayurbhanj Lok Sabha seat, was appointed MoS for Tribal Affairs and Jal Shakti. One may also add the appointment of veteran BJP leader Biswa Bhushan Harichandan as the Governor of Andhra Pradesh to the list of Odias who have been given prominent political positions by the Modi government.

Odisha's representation at the national level, however, has not been restricted to the political arena alone in the Modi regime. As principal secretary in the PMO, Pramod Kumar Mishra, an Odisha-born

IAS officer of the Gujarat cadre, is the most powerful bureaucrat in the present government. Girish Chandra Murmu, another Gujarat cadre IAS officer, is now the Comptroller and Auditor General of India (CAG). Before taking charge as CAG, Murmu, who served as principal secretary to Modi when he was the CM of Gujarat, was the first Lieutenant Governor (LG) of Jammu and Kashmir after it was made a union territory. He was Expenditure secretary in the Ministry of Finance when he was appointed LG. Tamil Nadu cadre IAS officer Shaktikant Das was the first Odia appointed as the Governor of the Reserve Bank of India (RBI) after his predecessor Urjit Patel resigned following differences with the central government. As Economic Affairs secretary in the Department of Finance, Das had done much of the firefighting in the messy aftermath of demonetization in November 2016.

There were several other Odias who have been appointed in key positions by the Modi dispensation. The more prominent among them are Justice Dipak Misra as the CJI, Dr Mrutyunjay Mohapatra as the director general (DG) of the India Meteorological Department, Dr Hrushikesh Senapati as the director of the National Council of Educational Research and Training, IPS officers Prakash Mishra as the DG of the Central Reserve Police Force and Dr Satya Narayan Pradhan first as the DG of the National Disaster Response Force and then as the head of the Narcotics Control Bureau, Adwaita Gadanayak as the DG of the National Gallery of Modern Art and Dr Kishor Chandra Basa as the chairperson of the National Monuments Authority.

It is possible that some of these appointments were made strictly on merit or as per seniority and had nothing to do with the fact that they were from Odisha, but the fact remains that Odisha never had it so good at the national level before. The special place that the state has in Modi's scheme of things is evident in other ways as well. Not since Independence have so many Odias received the Padma awards. Renowned sculptor the late Pandit Raghunath Mohapatra was conferred with the Padma Bhushan, while several other achievers were given the Padma Shri. They included Haladhar Nag, the eminent Koshali poet; Kamala Pujari, a tribal lady from Koraput who has done commendable work in preserving native paddy varieties; the late Prakash Rao, the Cuttack chaiwallah with a heart of gold who provided free education to over seventy poor slum children; and Daitari Nayak, Odisha's own Dasharath Majhi who single-handedly built a 3-kilometre canal to bring irrigation to his village in Keonjhar district.

Besides, many other grassroots-level achievers from the state have received generous praise from the PM on *Mann ki Baat*, his monthly radio address to the nation, making them celebrities overnight. Among them are Isak Munda, who took Odisha cuisine to the world through his YouTube channel (and earned huge money and fan following in the process); Biswatma Nayak, the co-founder of 'Chingari', a short video-sharing app touted as the Indian equivalent to the banned Chinese app, TikTok; Bijay Kumar Kabi, who created mangroves on 2 acres of land just outside his village; Amaresh Naresh Samanta, who has created several mini jungles around the port town of Paradeep; and Kuni Dehury, a girl from Keonjhar district who has initiated a revolution in the harnessing of solar energy in her area.

While Odias have started getting their long-delayed due at the national level at long last, nothing compares with the anointment of Murmu as the President of India. It marks the crowning glory for a state with immense potential that has been at the receiving end of central neglect and apathy for far too long.

# 14

# Cautious Optimism

While there is little doubt that the tribal society across India—from Gujarat to Meghalaya and from Rajasthan to Kerala—has hailed the elevation of Murmu to the highest constitutional post in the country, not every section is overly optimistic that it will make a material difference to the quality of their life. Some are hopeful, primarily on the basis of her record as the Governor of the predominantly tribal state of Jharkhand, that she will use her constitutional powers to ensure tribal rights and aspirations are not trampled upon. Others view her anointment as the President as mere tokenism and are less than sanguine if it will help improve the lot of the Adivasis.

'Dr A.P.J. Abdul Kalam was made the President. Did the lot of Muslims improve because of that? Ram Nath Kovind was made the President. Did it stop attacks on Dalits? So, why should we expect that the fate of the tribals will change after the elevation of Murmu as President?' asks Lalsingh Gamit, a prominent tribal leader in south Gujarat, while speaking to this author over the phone. Gamit is of the view that Murmu has been made President by the BJP government to legitimize the overturning of every law and constitutional provision in place to protect tribal rights. 'As you know, no Bill passed by Parliament can become law unless it is signed by the President. And in the parliamentary system that we have, the President has little option but to sign a Bill once it is passed by the legislature. True, s/he can return the Bill once. But if the government refuses to relent, s/he has no choice but to sign on the dotted line. So, the BJP government can enact all the anti-tribal laws it wants and then tell the tribals, "Look. The tribal President has signed it. Would she have signed it if it was not in your interest?"' says a cynical Gamit.

Gamit's views are echoed by Ranchi-based researcher and activist on tribal issues, Ashwini Pankaj. 'Murmu ji may be tribal. But all her political life, she has been a member of a party that is fundamentally anti-tribal. She may have her own views on issues concerning tribals, but she cannot be separated from the political philosophy that she subscribes to,' he says. But didn't Murmu stand up to the BJP government of the day as the Governor by stalling the amendments to the SNT and CNT Acts? 'No, she didn't. It was a compulsion for her because there were vociferous and widespread protests against the proposed amendments. There was no way she could have ignored that. Anyone in her place would have done the same,' says Pankaj, who has written the biography of Jaipal Singh Munda, the eminent tribal leader from Jharkhand who played a key role as a member of the Constituent Assembly in ensuring that tribal rights are protected in the Constitution.

Unlike Pankaj, Ranchi-based journalist and activist Dayamani Barla does give credit to Murmu for 'listening to the voice of the people' and returning the amendment Bills. But she also points to the formation of land banks, in gross violation of the provisions of the PESA Act, 1996, under her watch, as an indicator of the fact that she has not been equally decisive on other issues. 'The idea of land banks, which is essentially a move to usurp tribal land for corporates, is a negation of every law and constitutional provision in place to protect tribal land rights. And the Modi-led BJP government is determined to abolish or dilute every legal and constitutional provision that comes in the way of taking over tribal land. Take, for example, the Svamitva Yojana, which is a barely disguised move to take over all community assets of tribals like land, forest and water resources for the benefit of the corporates. It remains to be seen if Murmu ji can stop these moves that are bound to result in alienation of tribal land,' she told this author in an interview.

The ongoing takeover of tribal land and displacement of tribals to facilitate developmental projects is at the heart of the apprehensions of tribal leaders and activists that Murmu may not be able to stall such moves. Campaign for Survival and Dignity (CSD), Odisha, a coalition of organizations representing Adivasis and forest dwellers in the state, points to the Forest (Conservation) Rules, notified by the Union Ministry of Environment, Forests and Climate Change (MoEF & CC) on 29 June 2022 as the latest in a series of moves by the Centre to undermine tribal rights. The CSD has submitted a memorandum to the Centre and President Murmu calling for immediate withdrawal of the Rules, which strike at the very root of the Forest Rights Act (FRA), 2006, by doing away with the statutory requirement of taking consent from the Gram Sabha for diversion of forest land by the MoEF & CC, says CSD. 'The notification of Forest Rules, 2022 is clearly targeted to make it easier for project developers and private companies to take away forest land in violation of the rights of Adivasis and forest dwellers. It comes in the backdrop of a series of major legal changes either promulgated or proposed by the central government that seek to undermine and dilute the FRA and threaten the rights of Adivasis and forest dwellers,' says Gopinath Majhi, the convenor of the organization. 'The Adivasis have played a significant role in the protection and conservation of natural resources and biodiversity. The government must put an immediate end to this mindless diversion of precious natural resources, including thousands of hectares of forest land, and transfer the responsibilities of conserving and managing these resources to the Gram Sabha as envisaged under the PESA and the FRA,' adds Prafulla Samantara, eminent environmental activist and winner of the Goldman Environmental prize, considered the 'Green Nobel', in 2017.

Preservation of the tribal identity is the other area in which Murmu's role has come into sharp focus since her assumption of office as President. Tribal society is split down the middle on the question of whether her ascension to the Rashtrapati Bhavan is an assertion of the tribal identity or a dilution of it. While one section believes it is the best thing that has happened for the tribals since Independence, another section refuses to accept her as a 'true' representative of the tribals. Dr Krishna Chandra Tudu, academician and former head of TRL, Ranchi University, is among those who believe that her elevation as President will go a long way in changing the perception of tribals as an illiterate and uncivilized lot. 'After all, she is the first tribal outside Africa to occupy the highest post in a country,' he points out while speaking to this writer. Salkhan Murmu, two-time MP from Mayurbhanj and National President of Adivasi Sengal Abhiyan (ASA), concurs. 'It is a matter of great honour for tribals of India. Some people call it symbolism. But the significance of this act of symbolism should not be underestimated as it has given the tribals—not just in India but across the world—a new identity. As you can see, the hopes and aspirations of tribals are being talked about, discussed and debated as never before since she became President,' he told this biographer over the phone. Dr Rajat Kumar Kujur, who teaches political science and public administration in Sambalpur University, also believes that tribal issues will now come into greater focus not just in the media but in state legislatures as well as in Parliament because of her anointment as President.

But there is a fairly large section of tribals and those fighting for their rights that is not overly excited about Murmu becoming President or hopeful about the prospects of tribals getting a better deal on account of it. Their lack of enthusiasm stems primarily from their belief that she does not embody the essence of tribal society. Her unabashed and public display of allegiance to the Hindu way of life has not gone down well with many tribal leaders and activists. They insist that tribals are not Hindus and any attempt to brand them as such is an exercise aimed at diluting their tribal identity recognized and guaranteed by the founding fathers of the Indian constitution. 'The first thing she did after being named as the presidential candidate was to go to the local Shiva temple, sweep the temple floor and bow her head before Lord Shiva—in full public view and under the glare of TV cameras, mind you. What does that indicate? Why would tribals consider her their representative or expect much from her?' asks Ashwini Pankaj. 'Tribals are not fools. They can see through such games and understand who is doing the bidding of whom. It is obvious that she is being presented as a Hindutva icon as part of the BJP's agenda of ushering in a Hindu Rashtra,' adds Gamit.

Most tribal leaders this author talked to are of the firm view that tribals are not Hindus. They consider themselves a separate religion with a set of rituals, practices and belief systems distinct from the Hindu way of life. They refuse to be categorized as 'Others' in the Census and demand a separate column for themselves in the religion section of the decadal exercise. The Santhals of Jharkhand claim to profess the 'Sarna' religion, also known as the 'Adi Dharma', and have been pressing for a separate code for it in the Census. In November 2020, a special session of the Jharkhand Assembly was convened to pass a resolution demanding recognition of the Sarna religion and its inclusion as a separate code in the 2021 Census, but the Centre is yet to take a call on it.

While it is true that all tribals in India are nature worshippers, there is no denying the fact that not all of them follow the Sarna religion. The religious practices of tribals in Jharkhand are different from those followed by their counterparts in the Northeast. Even within a state, different tribes follow different religious practices and rituals. While conceding this point, Dr Kujur suggests that all tribes can be put under a column called Adi Dharma, or simply Adivasi, in the Census. The absence of such a provision is precisely what is facilitating religious conversion of tribals, he says.

History is witness to the fact that there have been organized efforts by non-tribals to divide tribals on the basis of religion since the colonial era, with the missionaries and the proponents of Hindutva engaged in a constant tug-of-war to win over the tribals. However, by and large, the tribal identity has prevailed over the religious identity of tribals. There is a reason the tribals have been allowed to retain their ST status even when they convert to another religion, says Dayamani Barla. But that has not stopped proponents of Hindutva from pressing for delisting of Adivasis who have converted to Christianity from the ST category. It will be a challenge for President Murmu to stop the forces out to divide tribals on religious basis, says Barla.

While acknowledging the role played by Murmu in the inclusion of the Santhali language in the Eighth Schedule of the Constitution, educated tribals say not much has happened since then to promote and popularize the language. The Central Sahitya Akademi has done nothing to promote the Santhali language, claims Dr K.C. Tudu. 'How many books have been published in the Santhali language by the Sahitya Akademi and other government institutions in the twenty years since its inclusion in the Eighth Schedule?' asks Ashwini Pankaj. Laxman Marandi, secretary of the council of the Rairangpur-based Adivasi Socio Educational and Cultural Association expects President Murmu to expedite the inclusion of the Santhali language in currency notes, which has been a long-standing demand of the tribals.

The expectations of tribals in the President's home district are more mundane. 'We are hopeful that the displacement of tribals to facilitate development projects and setting up of industries in our area will stop and the healthcare system in the district, which is in shambles at present, will improve. We also expect that the long-delayed railway expansion projects will finally be expedited now that one of our own is the President of the country,' says Ramachandra Murmu, a retired RBI officer from Mayurbhanj district now settled in Bhubaneswar.

The biggest expectation from President Murmu, however, is in enforcing the provisions of the Fifth and Sixth Schedules of the Constitution and in the proper implementation of specific laws aimed at protecting the rights of the tribals like the PESA Act and the FRA. Even those who are of the view that the scope for a President to do anything meaningful on his/her own is extremely limited in the parliamentary system of governance, we follow concede that there is a lot that a President can do in the specific area of the administration of Fifth and Sixth Schedule areas. The President, for example, has the powers to conduct an annual review of the administration of such areas as per the provisions of the Constitution and issue instructions to the state government, if they are not being followed in letter and spirit. But no President has bothered to exercise this power given by the Constitution, they point out, and assert that there is no reason to believe that President Murmu will be any different.

Not every tribal leader, however, is sceptical about President Murmu's willingness or ability to do her bit, especially in the enforcement of constitutional provisions in the Fifth and Sixth Schedule areas. Well-known tribal leader of Chhattisgarh and former Union Minister Arvind Netam, for one, is extremely hopeful that she will make a difference to the lives of tribals. Pointing to President Murmu's address on the occasion of Constitution Day on 26 November 2022, he says, 'It doesn't happen often that the President deviates from the written speech and speaks extempore. In doing so and pointing to the plight of the poor tribals languishing in jails for petty offences even after getting bail, President Murmu has dispelled the impression that she is going to be a "rubber stamp". In showing the mirror to the executive, legislature and the judiciary and asking them to introspect, she has proven that she is sensitive to the issues of tribals. And it has already had an immediate impact, as evident in the Supreme Court asking prison authorities across the country to submit details of such prisoners to the National Legal Services Authority within fifteen days so that a national policy could be framed for their release,' he told this author over the phone from Raipur. The President's intervention has kindled hope among the thousands of undertrial tribal prisoners in Chhattisgarh whose bail pleas have not been taken up for hearing for years, he adds.

Netam's views are shared by former MP Salkhan Murmu. 'With this one act, President Murmu has put the legislature, the executive and even the judiciary in the dock and awakened the nation to the sorry plight of undertrial tribal prisoners. I salute her for her courage. Tribals are extremely hopeful that something new, good and great is going to happen for them; that things which did not happen in the last seventy-five years will now happen,' he says in a telephonic conversation with this author.

There is little doubt that there was a political purpose behind the nomination of Murmu as its presidential candidate by the BJP, attracting the votes of tribals. And if the results of the Gujarat Assembly elections in December 2022, the first election held after Murmu became President, is any indication, the ruling party appears to have succeeded in its mission to a large extent. The party that had won just nine of the twenty-seven Assembly seats reserved for ST candidates in the last elections in 2017, won as many as twenty-four this time. BJP leaders claim that this is a result of the party's outreach to tribals with PM Modi speaking about the anointment of Murmu as the President in nearly every election meeting he addressed in the tribal belt. But political observers say it would be wrong to extrapolate the Gujarat election results and surmise that this will be replicated in all states with a sizeable tribal population in future elections. They point to the three-way split of the adivasi vote in Gujarat due to the entry to the Aam Aadmi Party in the election, which helped the BJP win a majority of seats in the tribal belt.

Dr Kujur is of the opinion that while tribals are happy that one of their own has become the President of the country, it is highly unlikely that they would vote for the party on a large scale only because of this. Local factors will influence their voting behaviour, he maintains. His views are echoed by Dr Tudu, who says, 'The tribals can see through the game being played by the BJP. Contrary to what the so-called elite believe, they understand the politics behind the act. They would not vote for a party that has followed anti-tribal policies in government just because a tribal has been made the President of the country.' Arvind Netam feels the BJP will not gain politically if it continues to follow policies that are against the interests of tribals. On his part, Salkhan Murmu says the ruling party will get the votes of tribals only if it finds a way of marrying the interests of tribals with its own political interests. 'The BJP will win the tribals over if it understands, honours and fulfills the aspirations of tribals,' he says. 'Why would a tribal bother who is the President when he is being forced to vacate his land to make way for an industrial project or sell it to pay the astronomical bill issued to him or her for non-existent power?' asks Dayamani Barla.

Shubhranshu Choudhury, the founder of the first community radio on mobile phone called CGNet Swara and the author of *Let's Call Him Vasu: With the Maoists in Chhattisgarh*, sums it up best saying there is cautious optimism among tribals after Murmu became the President. 'But it is unlikely to influence the voting preferences of tribals in a major way,' says the Chhattisgarh-based activist.

# Acknowledgements

The list of people I want to thank for their help, cooperation and words of encouragement in putting together this biography of President Droupadi Murmu—my first book—is too long to name each of them individually. However, I will be failing in my duty if I don't mention at least some of them, the ones who have gone out of their way to extend their unconditional and unstinted support to me in writing this book.

At the top of the list, of course, is my publisher, Penguin Random House, for giving me, a man with no published work except reports and articles in the media, the honour and opportunity of writing the first definitive biography of India's first tribal President. A special word of thanks is due to Chirag Thakkar, my commissioning editor, who has been extremely kind, understanding and patient through the process of writing the book even when I kept missing one deadline after another.

I am also grateful to Dangi Murmu, Gayamani Besra and Delha Soren—lifelong friends of the President—and Basudev Behera—her teacher in middle school—for providing me little-known and interesting vignettes from her childhood. Since there was precious little material on her early life available in the public domain, their inputs were invaluable in developing the narrative, especially in revisiting the President's childhood and adolescent years. I also thank retired IAS officer Santosh Satapathy, who was Principal Secretary to Murmu when she was the Governor of Jharkhand, for sharing anecdotes from the period which revealed some hitherto unknown facets of the President's persona.

Among the scores of political colleagues and contemporaries of President Murmu I talked to for this book, I would like to make special mention of senior BJP leader Manmohan Samal, senior BJD leader Debi Prasad Mishra, former CM of Jharkhand Babulal Marandi and Jharkhand Mukti Morcha general secretary Supriyo Bhattacharya for their valuable inputs.

I also express my gratitude to my good friend and colleague Ravi Prakash, the Ranchi-based senior journalist, for his immense help during my stay in the Jharkhand capital to meet people and gather material for the book. I could not have written the book without the help I received from J.P. Dash, who served as the private secretary to President Murmu when she was the Governor of Jharkhand, Bijay Kumar Nayak, private secretary to Murmu when she was a minister in the Odisha government who is now the additional press secretary to the President and Anil Kumar, my cousin and senior advocate in the Ranchi High Court.

Closer home, I am grateful to senior Rairangpur-based journalist Nigamananda Patnaik for putting me in touch with his extensive contacts in the President's home district and for giving me all his time during my stay in the President's home town to collect material for the book. My good friends from Baripada, Shivaji Moulik and Kalyan Kumar Sinha, too, deserve my gratitude for their help and inputs in writing the book.

Right through the process of writing this book, veteran Ahmedabad-based journalist Nachiketa Desai, who is like an elder brother to me, has been a constant source of encouragement. His words spurred me to move ahead with renewed vigour whenever the pace slackened. It is such a pity he did not live long enough to see the publication of the book.

Last but not least, I am indebted to my wife, Bharati, for constantly pushing and prodding me since I began working on this biography.

# Notes

## Chapter 1: Destiny's Daughter

1. 'Census India 2011 - Population of India', Census India, https://www.censusindia2011.com (Accessed February 12, 2023).

## Chapter 2: The Belated Birthday Gift

1. Narendra Modi, Twitter post, June 21, 2022, 9.52 p.m., https://twitter.com/i/web/status/153928255519877 1201?lang=en (Accessed February 12, 2023).
2. 'Droupadi Murmu as NDA presidential candidate: It is a proud moment for Odisha, says CM Naveen Patnaik', *Economic Times*, June 23, 2022, https://bit.ly/3RQpXBL (Accessed February 12, 2023).
3. 'Mom's Hard Work, Integrity Have Taken Her to Where She Is Today, says Droupadi Murmu's Daughter', *Times of India*, June 24, 2022, https://timesofindia.indiatimes.com/city/bhubaneswar/moms-hard-work-integrity-have-taken-her-to-where-she-is-today-says-

droupadi-murmus-daughter/articleshow/92425342. cms (Accessed February 12, 2023).

4. '13-Yr-Old Pens Book on Draupadi Murmu', https:// www.thehansindia.com/hans/young-hans/13-yr-old-pens-book-on-draupadi-murmu-754377 (Accessed February 18, 2023).

## Chapter 3: The Masterstroke

1. 'Census India 2011 - Population of India', Census India, https://www.censusindia2011.com (Accessed February 18, 2023).

2. Lalit Sharma, 'Shiromani Akali Dal Announces Support for NDA's Presidential Nominee Droupadi Murmu', *India Today*, July 1, 2022, indiatoday.in/india/story/ shiromani-akali-dal-extends-support-nda-presidential-nominee-droupadi-murmu-1969152-2022-07-01 (Accessed March 17, 2023).

3. '"Kept Rakhi Promise": NDA Presidential Pick on Naveen Patnaik Support', NDTV, July 8, 2022, https:// www.ndtv.com/india-news/kept-rakhi-promise-nda-presidential-pick-on-naveen-patnaik-support-3140098 (Accessed March 17, 2023).

4. 'Odisha Congress to Not Back "Daughter of Soil" Murmu for Presidential Election, Claims She Believes in BJP-RSS Ideology', *Outlook*, June 23, 2022, https:// www.outlookindia.com/national/odisha-congress-to-not-back-daughter-of-soil-murmu-for-presidential-election-claims-she-believes-in-bjp-rss-ideology-news-204252 (Accessed March 17, 2023).

5. 'The Tribes of Odisha', https://www.scstrti.in/index. php/communities/tribes (Accessed March 17, 2023).

6. 'After Sharad Pawar, Farooq Abdullah Turns Down Offer to Be Opposition's Presidential Candidate', *India Today*, June 18, 2022, https://www.indiatoday.

in/india/story/farooq-abdullah-turns-down-offer-joint-opposition-candidate-presidential-election-sharad-pawar-mamata-banerjee-1963966-2022-06-18 (Accessed March 17, 2023).

7. Sharad Pawar, 6.46 p.m., June 15, 2022, https://twitter.com/PawarSpeaks/status/1537061489873330176 (Accessed February 18, 2023).

8. Aditi Tandon, '"Honoured but..." Gopalkrishna Gandhi Declines Opposition Request to contest Presidential Polls', *Tribune*, https://www.tribuneindia.com/news/nation/honoured-but-gopalkrishna-gandhi-declines-opposition-request-to-contest-presidential-polls-405473 (Accessed February 16, 2023).

9. 'A Consensus Could Have Been Built on Murmu: Mamata Banerjee', *Times of India*, July 2, 2022, https://timesofindia.indiatimes.com/india/a-consensus-could-have-been-built-on-murmu-mamata-banerjee/articleshow/92606494.cms (Accessed February 18, 2023).

10. 'Country Does Not Need "Rubber Stamp" President, Says Yashwant Sinha', NDTV, June 30, 2022, https://www.ndtv.com/india-news/country-does-not-need-rubber-stamp-president-says-yashwant-sinha-3113536 (Accessed February 18, 2023).

11. 'Droupadi Murmu Represents "Evil Philosophy of India": Congress Leader Ajoy Kumar', *Times of India*, July 13, 2022, https://timesofindia.indiatimes.com/videos/toi-original/droupadi-murmu-represents-evil-philosophy-of-india-congress-leader-ajoy-kumar/videoshow/92858946.cms (Accessed February 18, 2023).

12. 'Don't Want Statue in President House: Tejashwi Yadav Takes a Dig at NDA's Prez Pick Droupadi Murmu', *India Today*, July 17, 2022, https://www.indiatoday.

in/india/story/dont-want-statue-president-house-rjd-tejashwi-yadav-nda-president-candidate-droupadi-murmu-1976590-2022-07-17 (Accessed February 18, 2023).

13. 'Murmu Makes it to Raisina Hill after Sangma and Swell Failed to Do So', July 21, 2022, http://www.uniindia.com/news/east/election-meghalaya-tribals/2784596.html (Accessed February 18, 2023).

14. Neha Singh, '10 Years Ago, Late PA Sangma "Dreamt" of Tribal Indian President...but Now It's a "Reality"', Newsroom Post, July 22, 2022, https://newsroompost.com/india/10-years-ago-late-pa-sangma-dreamt-of-tribal-president-of-india-but-now-its-a-reality/5144112.html (Accessed February 18, 2023).

15. 'Address by Smt. Droupadi Murmu on her assumption of office as President of India', PIB Delhi, July 25, 2022, https://pib.gov.in/PressReleasePage.aspx?PRID=1844557 (Accessed February 18, 2023).

16. Gery Shih, 'In a First, India Elects Tribal Woman to be President', *Washington Post*, July 21, 2022, https://www.washingtonpost.com/world/2022/07/21/india-president-tribal/ (Accessed February 18, 2023).

17. Raj Chengappa and Romita Dutta, 'Tribal Power', *India Today*, August 4, 2022.

## Chapter 4: 'Puti' to Droupadi

1. Kamya Kadambini, YouTube, https://youtu.be/VwLapZbC9h0 (Accessed February 18, 2023).

2. 'Sex Ratio in India', Population Census, https://www.census2011.co.in/sexratio.php (Accessed February 19, 2023).

3. Kaushik Dekka, 'A Status Report', in 'Tribal Tribute', *India Today*, August 8, 2022.

4.  Quoted from a *Sambad* report in Tejaswini Panda, *Droupadi Murmu-Odia Asmitara Pratika* (Droupadi Murmu: A Symbol of Odia pride), (Bhubaneswar: Timepass Publications, 2022), p. 72.

5.  Facebook, https://www.facebook.com/KanakNews/videos/1394625384353132/?extid=WA-UNK-UNK-UNK-AN_GK0T-GK1C-GK2C (Accessed February 18, 2023).

## Chapter 7: Political Plunge

1.  'Bapa Thile Sardar', in Pandit Daitari Mahapatra, *Kalinga Kanya Droupadi Murmu* (Cuttack: Uma Books, 2022).

2.  'Bangiriposi-Gorumahisani Railway Link Yet to Take Off', *New Indian Express*, January 2, 2017, https://www.newindianexpress.com/states/odisha/2017/jan/02/bangiriposi-gorumahisani-railway-link-yet-to-take-off-1555250.html (Accessed 19 February 2023).

## Chapter 8: Tragic Turn

1.  Before going to bed, the deities are decorated with 'Bastra Shringar' (dress), 'Bhushan Shringar' (ornaments) and finally 'Pushpa Shringar' (flowers). The last one, which happens just before the deities retire, is called the 'Bada Singhara Besha' in temple parlance.

2.  'Simplicity, Thy Name is Droupadi Murmu', *Times of India*, July 22, 2022.

## Chapter 9: People's Governor

1.  'The Tribes of Odisha', https://www.scstrti.in/index.php/communities/tribes (Accessed March 17, 2023).

2.  'Jharkhand Population - Census India 2011', Census India, https://www.censusindia2011.com/jharkhand-population.html (Accessed March 1, 2023).

3.  'Jharkhand Population: Census India 2011', https://
    www.censusindia2011.com/jharkhand-population.
    html (Accessed March 23, 2023).

4.  The draft of the Chotanagpur Tenancy Act
    (Amendment), Bill, 2016: Sec. 2.

5.  Constituent Assembly of India: Excluded and partially
    excluded areas (Other than Assam) Sub Committee.
    Vol. I: Report, https://dspace.gipe.ac.in/xmlui/handle/
    10973/49677 (Accessed March 1, 2023).

6.  'The Pathalgadi Rebellion', *The Hindu*, April 18, 2018,
    https://www.thehindu.com/news/national/other-states/
    the-pathalgadi-rebellion/article23530998.ece (Accessed
    March 17, 2023).

7.  Every university has a syndicate that takes all important
    decisions with regard to the university.

8.  Brig. Advitya Madan (retd), 'An Inspirational Date with
    Droupadi Murmu', *Hindustan Times*, July 21, 2022,
    https://www.hindustantimes.com/cities/chandigarh-
    news/an-inspirational-date-with-droupadi-murmu-
    101658347221522.html (Accessed March 1, 2023).

## Chapter 10: Commoner Again

1.  'Kholakotha | Earlier Discussion with Former Jharkhand
    Governor Draupadi Murmu', YouTube, https://www.
    youtube.com/watch?v=lcgnWrpo8j0 (Accessed March
    17, 2023).

## Chapter 11: President Murmu

1.  'Address by Smt. Droupadi Murmu on her assumption of
    office as President of India', PIB, President's Secretariat,
    July 25, 2022, https://pib.gov.in/PressReleasePage.
    aspx?PRID=1844557 (Accessed March 2, 2023).

2.  'Address by Smt. Droupadi Murmu on Her Assumption
    of Office as President of India', https://pib.gov.in/

PressReleasePage.aspx?PRID=1844557    (Accessed March 17, 2023).

3.  Shruti Shende, 'Lores of the Loom', PressReader.com, August 2, 2022, https://www.pressreader.com/india/ht-city/20220802/281840057424347 (Accessed March 17, 2023).

4.  'Address to the Nation by Hon'ble President of India Smt. Droupadi Murmu on the Eve of the 76th Independence Day', PIB Delhi, President's Secretariat, August 14, 2022, https://pib.gov.in/PressReleasePage.aspx?PRID=1851827 (Accessed March 2, 2023).

5.  'Uproar over Adhir's Remark on President Murmu: Top 10 Developments in Parliament Today', *Indian Express*, July 28, 2022, https://indianexpress.com/article/india/parliament-top-10-developments-adhir-chowdhury-murmu-rashtrapatni-smriti-irani-8056584/ (Accessed March 2, 2023).

6.  Ibid.

7.  Ibid.

8.  'No Country Should Get such President: Congress Leader Stokes Controversy', *Deccan Herald*, October 6, 2022,
    https://www.deccanherald.com/national/national-politics/no-country-should-get-such-president-congress-leader-stokes-controversy-1151085.html (Accessed March 2, 2023).

9.  '"Anti-Tribal mindset": BJP Blasts Congress Leader for Attack on President Murmu', *India Today*, October 6, 2022, https://www.indiatoday.in/india/story/anti-tribal-mindset-bjp-blasts-congress-leader-udit-raj-for-attacking-president-murmu-2008885-2022-10-06 (Accessed March 17, 2023).

10. Poulami Ghosh, 'Udit Raj Regrets Remarks on Droupadi Murmu, but Says "I have a right"', *Hindustan*

*Times,* October 7, 2022, https://www.hindustantimes. com/india-news/udit-raj-regrets-remarks-on-droupadi-murmu-but-says-i-have-a-right-101665106130166. html (Accessed March 17, 2023).

11. 'West Bengal Minister Akhil Giri's Comments on President Murmu Draws Criticism', *The Hindu,* November 12, 2022, https://www.thehindu.com/news/ national/other-states/bjp-seeks-dismissal-of-west-bengal-minister-akhil-giri-for-his-remarks-on-president-murmu/article66127800.ece (Accessed March 17, 2023).

12. 'BJP Seeks Akhil Giri's Dismissal from West Bengal Govt over Remarks on President Droupadi Murmu', *Financial Express,* November 12, 2022, https://www. financialexpress.com/india-news/bjp-seeks-akhil-giris-dismissal-from-west-bengal-govt-over-remarks-on-president-droupadi-murmu/2809845/ (Accessed March 2, 2023).

13. 'Odisha Angry over Remarks on President Murmu', *Times of India,* November 13, 2022.

14. 'Furore in Odisha over Ahkhil Giri's Comment on Prez Murmu, Parties Unite in Demand for His Arrest', *New Indian Express,* November 13, 2022, https:// www.newindianexpress.com/states/odisha/2022/ nov/13/furore-in-odisha-over-akhil-giris-comment-on-prez-murmu-parties-unite-in-demand-for-his-arrest-2517840.html (Accessed March 17, 2023).

15. 'Bengal Minister Akhil Giri Faces Backlash for Comment on Murmu, Apologises', *Indian Express,* November 14, 2022, https://indianexpress.com/article/cities/kolkata/ tmc-minister-akhil-giri-president-droupadi-murmu-comments-8264076/ (Accessed March 17, 2023).

16. Suman Mandal, 'TMC Minister Akhil Giri Apologises for His Comments against President Droupadi Murmu', *Times of India,* November 12, 2022, https://

timesofindia.indiatimes.com/city/kolkata/tmc-minister-akhil-giri-apologises-for-his-comments-against-president-droupadi-murmu/articleshow/95469264.cms (Accessed March 17, 2023).

17. 'Mamata Banerjee Condemns Akhil Giri's Remarks On President Droupadi Murmu', *Outlook*, November 14, 2022, https://www.outlookindia.com/national/mamata-banerjee-condemns-akhil-giri-s-remarks-on-president-droupadi-murmu-news-237356 (Accessed April 3, 2023).

## Chapter 12: Homecoming

1. Debabrata Mohapatra, 'Odisha: "Mahaprasad" from Puri Temple May Be Sent to Rashtrapati Bhavan', *Times of India*, November 12, 2022, https://timesofindia.indiatimes.com/city/bhubaneswar/mahaprasad-from-puri-temple-may-be-sent-to-rashtrapati-bhavan/articleshow/95463732.cms (Accessed March 17, 2023).

2. *Dharitri*, November 12, 2022.

3. Hemanta Pradhan, 'Odisha: On School Return, President Droupadi Murmu Takes Trip Down Memory Lane', *Times of India*, November 12, 2022, https://timesofindia.indiatimes.com/city/bhubaneswar/on-school-return-droupadi-takes-trip-down-memory-lane/articleshow/95463744.cms (Accessed March 17, 2023).

## Chapter 13: Odisha's Finest Hour

1. Odisha Tourism, https://odishatourism.gov.in/content/tourism/en/discover/attractions/buddhist-sites/jeerango.html (Accessed March 2, 2023).

2. Department of Steel & Mines, Government of Odisha, https://odishaminerals.gov.in/ (Accessed March 2, 2023).

# Index